JESUS

AMONG OTHER GODS

The Absolute Claims *of* the Christian Message

Ravi Zacharias

W Publishing Group™

www.wpublishinggroup.com

A Division of Thomas Nelson, Inc.
www.ThomasNelson.com

Library of Congress Cataloging-in-Publication Data

Zacharias, Ravi K.
    Jesus among other gods / by Ravi Zacharias.
       p. cm.
    ISBN 0-8499-1437-X (hardcover)
    ISBN 0-8499-4327-2 (trade paper)
    ISBN 0-8499-4263-2 (international edition)
       1. Apologetics. 2. Christianity and other religions. I. Title.
    BT1230 .Z33 2000
    239—dc21
                                                                         00–039920
                                                                              CIP

Printed in the United States of America

02 03 04 05 06 PHX 9 8 7 6 5

To the memory of two very dear friends

Charles Kip Jordon
and
Robert Earl Fraley

Both had a share in this effort;
Kip greatly encouraged me to write the book.
Robert made sure I took the time to write it.

None of us knew how soon they would be with Him
Who is the focus of this work.

CONTENTS

ACKNOWLEDGMENTS

WITH THE SUPPORTIVE HELP OF MANY, THIS BOOK FINALLY TOOK SHAPE. I express my heartfelt gratitude to them all.

Danielle DuRant, as always, provided invaluable research support and took on the tedious task of tracking down sources.

Editors Jan Dennis and Jennifer Stair smoothed the bumps significantly.

Laura Kendall with W Publishing Group drew it together at the end. To the leadership at W Publishing Group—David Moberg, Joey Paul, Rob Birkhead, and others—I express my sincere thanks for their gracious words of encouragement.

Finally and most importantly, my thanks to my wife, Margie. She pored over every page with the utmost scrutiny to make her suggestions that make it more readable. I gladly allow her the last word.

This book comes as an expression of a heart grateful to God for all that He has done in my own life.

INTRODUCTION

WHEN I BEGAN WRITING THIS BOOK, I LITTLE DREAMED OF HOW difficult a task this was going to be.

The difficulty has really not been in knowing what to say, but in knowing what *not* to say. We are living in a time when sensitivities are at the surface, often vented with cutting words. Philosophically, you can believe anything, so long as you do not claim it to be true. Morally, you can practice anything, so long as you do not claim that it is a "better" way. Religiously, you can hold to anything, so long as you do not bring Jesus Christ into it. If a spiritual idea is eastern, it is granted critical immunity; if western, it is thoroughly criticized. Thus, a journalist can walk into a church and mock its carryings on, but he or she dare not do the same if the ceremony is from the eastern fold. Such is the mood at the end of the twentieth century.

A mood can be a dangerous state of mind, because it can crush reason under the weight of feeling. But that is precisely what I believe postmodernism best represents—a mood.

How does one in a mood such as this communicate the message of Jesus Christ, in which truth and absoluteness are not only assumed, but also sustained?

Well, for starters, let us be sure that Jesus was not western. In fact, some of His parables were so eastern that I think much of the West may not have entered into the rigor and humor of what He said. What has happened in the West is that His impact over the centuries has been so felt that the ethos and moral impetus of His message changed the course of western civilization. The western naturalist, in sheer arrogance, does not see this. Now, after technological progress, wealth and enterprise have so woven themselves around the message of Jesus that popular models of Christianity appear as nothing more than self and greed at the center, with strands of Christian thought at the periphery. This adulteration has rightly merited the severe rebuke of the critic. We would do well to remember, however, what Augustine said: We are never to judge a philosophy by its abuse. That aside, the way Jesus spoke, the proverbs and stories that He told, and the very context in which He addressed issues was steeped in an eastern idiom. Let us not forget that.

But if the western world has been guilty of adulterating His message beyond recognition, the eastern world has often forgotten that it has, by fault, left a mass of religious belief, sometimes bizarre, irresponsibly uncriticized. Take, for example, various forms of eastern worship and practice. During the writing of this book, I happened to be at several such settings. In one of these, devotees had a large number of hooks pierced into their bodies. Knives were pierced through their faces and small spears through their tongues. Sights like these terrify visitors and children. One has to ask, Why do the same thinkers who criticize any western forms of spirituality not take this to task?

Closer to home, we see the writings of Deepak Chopra, who teaches a doctrine of spirituality, success, and prosperity woven into Vedaic teachings, karma, and self-deification. By contrast, we see millions devoted to that underlying world-view living in abject poverty. Have they somehow missed the mark? What is wrong with the picture here? One can readily see that every religion must face the responsibility of answering the questions posed to it.

Numerous other issues can be raised, but the point remains the same.

As a result of all this, serious distortions have come into vogue. Some proponents of other religious faiths talk about the "myth of Christian uniqueness." Others have demanded that propagation of one's faith is wrong and that "conversion" should be banned.

Such a mood brings a tyranny all its own.

The reality is that if religion is to be treated with intellectual respect, then it must stand the test of truth, regardless of the mood of the day. This book is a defense of the uniqueness of the Christian message.

As I have drawn it to a close, I wish I could have said more and argued more by contrast, but the current mood may not lend itself to any more than this.

The route I have followed is to present a clear difference between Jesus and any other claimant to divinity or prophetic status. I have taken six questions that Jesus answered in a way that none other would have answered. An opponent may disagree with His answers, but when those answers are all added up, antagonists will not be able to challenge His uniqueness. I believe every answer is fascinating, and I wish I could have done justice to them. As it stands, the chapters were becoming lengthier, as the subjects had to be adequately dealt with.

The difficulty in containing the length was exacerbated by the fact that I also needed to contrast the answers with those of other leading religions. By far, the most difficult one to deal with was the question posed to Jesus on pain and suffering. That chapter I have divided into three parts.

The final chapter is not a question posed to Jesus, but a question posed on His behalf, to His followers and to His doubters. It was only fitting to end it that way.

As you will soon note, I have not given His answers in distinction to every religion that offers answers on such matters. I have only dealt with those that still draw a large following around the world—Islam, Hinduism, and Buddhism.

I must say one other thing. I have covered thousands of miles during this writing, not only for the book, but also through invitations to speak in various parts of the world. I have walked through temples, mosques, and other religious sites. I have spoken to students at universities in which the predominant religion is not Christian. In the course of this, I have met some very fine and gracious people. By nature, I am a people person. I enjoy conversations, especially around a meal with newfound friends. One such person was the room attendant at a hotel where I was staying. He is a Muslim man. Every day when he came in to make up my room, he would also make me a cup of tea, and we would talk. On his off day, he took me sightseeing in his city, and we visited many places of worship. I will never forget him. I wish more people showed the kindness that he did and the courtesies he always offered.

And that is the point I wish to make. We can be world-views apart without anger and offense. What I believe, I believe very seriously. And it is because of this that I write the book. By equal measure, anything to the contrary, I must question.

My earnest prayer is that when you read this, you will make your judgment of the Christian message based on truth, not the mood of our times. Moods change. Truth does not.

Chapter One

CLIMBING A MASSIVE WALL

I BEGIN WITH AN INCIDENT IN MY LIFE THAT CAUSES STORMS OF emotion to well up within me. Some memories are easy to relive. Others, even with the passage of time, when recalled again, throb like a reinjured wound. For that reason alone I find this, of all my past memories, very difficult to retell. It is only because the intervening years have helped me to look beyond the earlier hurts that I am able to bring this long-past moment into the present. But more than that, this sad happening, alongside a handful of others, may well have begun my journey toward God by bringing me to a screeching halt and forcing me to ask myself some hard questions.

I was sixteen years old and a student in a community college because it provided a shortcut to finishing high school. One day after classes normally ended, I was cycling back home, little suspecting what lay ahead of me. It had been a routine day from my point of view, as normal as any other. But this one was going to end differently.

As I turned into our backyard, I saw a sight that was most unusual. Normally my father would not even be home at this time, but there he was, standing at the door with his arms stretched across the open doorway as if to block my entry into the house. I greeted him with a furtive glance, and he made no reply. I felt his eyes bearing down on me, which spelled terror into my heart.

My relationship with my father left a lot to be desired, and my aimless life was a cause of immense frustration to him. I can candidly say that I feared him in ways that to this day I am not sure I fully understand. This was a moment I will never forget.

"How was school?" he asked.

It was a question he had never asked before. My report card usually answered that question, giving rise to the resulting tense discussions. I should have known he had a reason for asking this day, but without any suspicion I answered, "Fine."

His exact language that followed would be hard to repeat, but the torrent of anger he unleashed on me and the thrashing I received left me trembling and sobbing. Had my mother not intervened, I could have been seriously hurt. My charade was over. A game I had foolishly played had come to a very bitter end, with no one the winner.

The truth is that I had not been at school that day. In fact, I had not been there for some time. I had spent my days wandering the streets on my bicycle in search of a cricket match I could watch or even perhaps take part in. Absent from classes, I would show up for the exams and squeak through. How I expected to get away with this ruse I will never know. But wrong-doing has a way of robbing one even of common sense.

Why had all this happened in the first place? One might think the whole episode merely indicated a passionate dislike for school. But there was far more than just that. No one who knew me would have ever suspected the depths of emptiness within me. I was one of those teenagers who struggled with much on the inside but did not know where to turn for answers. For that matter, I did not know if answers to my deepest hungers actually even existed. Was everyone I met in life facing the same degree of questioning and just masking it better? Or was skepticism the realm of just a hapless few? Putting it plainly, life, to me, just did not make sense. All the pent-up longings put together added up to nothing but a wish that had no possibility of fulfillment. Jean Paul Sartre's description of life as a useless passion seemed perfectly appropriate. That confrontation with my dad probably summed up all that was tearing me apart on the inside.

That night, I stood punished and facing a wall. It may well have been a fitting metaphor of my life. My most pressing struggles had imprisoned me, and in those hours, laden with remorse, I wondered how I would ever break free to breathe the fresh air of a life unshackled.

Oscar Wilde's poem "The Ballad of Reading Gaol," which was written from prison, says it well:

> I never saw sad men who looked
> With such a wistful eye
> Upon that little tent of blue
> We prisoners call the sky,
> And at every careless cloud that passed
> In happy freedom by.

I was one of those "sad men," although I never showed it. I had that wistful yearning to be free. Thus, as grim as that evening was, it put in perspective the walls that seemed immovable. I had to look reality in the face if I was ever to find a way to understand it.

The intense soul search that began that night was ultimately to lead me to the person of Jesus Christ. How that happened in a culture that is rigorously pantheistic and (at least on paper) religiously all-encompassing is a miracle in itself. I would like to trace some of those steps for you.

SEEING MILESTONES IN RETROSPECT

Selecting defining moments is not an easy task. In a rigorous effort to be both fair and realistic, I have looked at some of the road marks I have crossed and wish to bring you to the starting point of my reasoning. From a chronological perspective, one might misconstrue the sequence as an experience that led to an argument. But looking back down the road years later, I can see that logically, the argument preceded, and with time, was sustained by the experience. This opening chapter, therefore, begins with my story, but the following chapters will stand on the argument.

The purpose of this book is to lay out for you, the reader, why I firmly believe Jesus Christ to be who He claimed to be—the Son of the living God, the One who came to seek and to save a lost humanity. At a time in our cultural history when the West is looking more like the East and the East is covertly trying to emulate the West, this is much needed. Religions are making a revival, but often as a hybrid of western marketing techniques and eastern mythology—a devastating combination of seduction through media and mysticism. The first casualty in such a mix is truth, and, consequently, the person of God.

Yet if the human spirit is to survive and every legitimate discipline to find fruitful expression, truth cannot be sacrificed at the altar of a pretended tolerance. All religions, plainly and simply, cannot be true. Some beliefs are false, and we know them to be false. So it does no good to put a halo on the notion of tolerance as if everything could be equally true. To deem all beliefs equally true is sheer nonsense for the simple reason that to deny that statement would also, then, be true. But if the denial of the statement is also true, then all religions are not true.

In the real-life struggles between right and wrong, justice and injustice, life and death, we all realize that truth does matter. Jesus Christ repeatedly talked about the supreme value of truth. While His life has been scrutinized more than any other's, it is remarkable that even skeptics have granted and recognized His unparalleled life and impact. Here, for example, is an opinion from a highly respected scholar, the famed historian W. E. H. Lecky:

> The character of Jesus has not only been the highest pattern of virtue, but the strongest incentive in its practice, and has exerted so deep an influence, that it may be truly said that the simple record of three years of active life has done more to regenerate and to soften mankind than all the disquisitions of philosophers and all the exhortations of moralists.[1]

Historians, poets, philosophers—and a host of others—have regarded Him as the centerpiece of history. He Himself made a statement that was very dramatic and daring when He said to the apostle Thomas, "I am the way and the truth and the life. No one comes to the Father except through me" (John 14:6). Every word of that statement challenges the fundamental beliefs of the Indian culture from which I come, and in reality, actually stands against an entire world today.

Just look at the implicit claims in that statement. First and foremost, He asserted that there is only one way to God. That shocks postmodern moods and mind-sets. Hinduism and Bahaism have long challenged the concept of a single way to God. The Hindu religion, with its multifaceted belief system, vociferously attacks such exclusivity.

Jesus also unequivocally stated that God is the Author of life and that meaning in life lies in coming to Him. This assertion would be categorically denied by Buddhism, which is a nontheistic if not atheistic religion.

Jesus revealed Himself as the Son of God who led the way to the Father. Islam considers that claim to be blasphemous. How can God have a Son?

Jesus claimed that we can personally know God and the absolute nature of His truth. Agnostics deny that possibility.

One can go down the line and see that every claim that Jesus made of Himself challenged my culture's most basic assumptions about life and meaning. (It is important to remember, of course, that these basic religions within the Indian framework are also not in concert with each other. Buddha was a Hindu before he rejected some of Hinduism's fundamental doctrines and conceived in their place the Buddhist way. Islam radically differs from Hinduism.)

Ironically, it was that same apostle, Thomas, to whom Jesus spoke these words, who took the exclusive claims of Christ to India and paid for the gospel message with his life.

Was Jesus who He claimed to be? Is the Christian claim to uniqueness a myth? Can one study the life of Christ and demonstrate conclusively that He was and is the way, the truth, and the life? That is the question I propose to answer in this book. I believe there is overwhelming evidence to support Jesus' claims. I begin with my personal story only to put into context how my own journey began and how I arrived at the conclusion that Jesus is who He said He is.

A Perilous Glance

There is, understandably, in these preliminary thoughts a personal uncertainty. How do I say what I want to say without bringing hurt to anyone else or, for that matter, to any culture? This is hard. Home and culture are the treasured cradles in which one is nurtured. I find myself torn out of love for the truth and the cost of candor.

The hazard in such an undertaking struck me some months ago as I read the powerful book *Into Thin Air* by Jon Krakauer. The author recounts the ascent to Mount Everest by a team of climbers of which he was a part. I noted with empathy his anguished apology at the end of the book to many of the family members of those who lost their lives in the ascent, prompted by the errors he had made in some of his first stated recollections. Writing so soon after the tragedy found him erroneously recalling details that he later had to retract or correct. He conceded that had he waited before penning his account, he would have been less prone to such mistakes.

But there was more, and therein lay the rub. Some of what he had said reflected poorly not just on him, but on the character or efforts of others. For that he was truly sorry. This latter mistake is very serious, for one's own life may be laid bare at personal cost, but not at the cost of someone else's sacred trust. To that caution I shall pay close heed, and if I have failed, it is only because to suppress the incidents would be to distort the truth of my struggle.

I can now enjoy the benefit of time's distant view. The Jesus I know and love today I encountered at the age of seventeen. But His name and His tug in my life mean infinitely more now than they did when I first surrendered my life to Him. I came to Him because I did not know which way to turn. I have remained with Him because there is no other way I wish to turn. I came to Him longing for something I did not have. I remain with Him because I have something I will not trade. I came to Him as a stranger. I remain with Him in the most intimate of friendships. I came to Him unsure about the future. I remain with Him certain about my destiny. I came amid the thunderous cries of a culture that has three hundred and thirty million deities. I remain with Him knowing that truth cannot be all-inclusive. Truth by definition excludes.

You hear it a thousand times and more growing up in the East—"We all come through different routes and end up in the same place." But I say to you, God is not a place or an experience or a feeling. Pluralistic cultures are beguiled by the cosmetically courteous idea that sincerity or privilege of birth is all that counts and that truth is subject to the beholder. In no other discipline of life can one be so naive as to claim inherited belief or insistent belief as the sole determiner of truth. Why, then, do we make the catastrophic error of thinking that all religions are right and that it does not matter whether the claims they make are objectively true?

All religions are not the same. All religions do not point to God. All religions *do not say* that all religions are the same. At the heart of *every* religion is an uncompromising commitment to a particular way of defining who God is or is not and accordingly, of defining life's purpose.

Anyone who claims that all religions are the same betrays not only an ignorance of all religions but also a caricatured view of even the best-known ones. Every religion at its core is exclusive.

But the concept of "many ways" was absorbed subliminally in my life as a youngster. I was conditioned into that way of thinking before I found out its smuggled prejudices. It took years to find out that the cry for openness is never what it purports to be. What the person means by saying, "You must be open to everything" is really, "You must be open to everything that I am open to, and anything that I disagree with, you must disagree with too."

Indian culture has that veneer of openness, but it is highly critical of anything that hints at a challenge to it. It is no accident that within that so-called tolerant culture was birthed the caste system. All-inclusive philosophies can only come at the cost of truth. And no religion denies its core beliefs.

Within such systemic relativism, one tends to drift and float with the cultural tide and give no thought to the unforgiving nature of reality. That is how life is lived out in pantheistic cultures. No doubt, there is a wealth of thought that has built an impressive culture for more than one billion people, a culture that has defied economic privation, political turmoil, and religious hostilities, existing in the words of its people as "Mother India."

One does not have the advantage of choosing where one is born. Yet the words of the poet—"Breathes there the man with soul so dead, Who never to himself has said, 'This is my own, my native land'"[2]—ring wrenchingly true. In that cultural air, my life, my language, and my values were shaped and tested. I will ever be grateful for that privilege and for the treasured gifts it bestowed on me. The songs, the language, and the dreams it lodged in me I hope I never outlive. But a search for the one true God in a land full of gods is a very daunting task. Religion has a checkered history, and some of it is reprehensible.

An inheritor of the complexity of this culture, I grew up with walls of quiet desperation gradually building within me that moved me moment by moment to a point of personal crisis. I have heard it said that every weakness in a capable person is generally a strength abused. The same applies to culture. In the context of my upbringing, the abuses of those strengths of culture confirmed that adage.

Vulnerability in Strength

First and foremost is the strength of the nuclear family. As I knew it, the culture is strong and commendably reverential of the immediate family. The bonds of the household are wrapped tightly in India. But that strength becomes easily vulnerable to abuse. Many parents seem to seek to relive their lives through their children, and the success of the children socially elevates the family. Individuality is swallowed up by the clan. Every day, hundreds of advertisements are printed across the newspapers of the land in what is called the matrimonial section—parents looking for spouses for their children. Every prospective bride and groom is advertised as being from "a good home" and searching for someone from "a good home." "My son is an engineer." "My daughter is a doctor." "My son stood first in his class." "My daughter won a scholarship abroad." So run the boasts at social gatherings. Everything is done to keep the family as a single unit, with reverence for the parents' wishes on everything from jobs to marriage.

For me, the strength of the home was also the soil for the seeds of loneliness growing within. It centered on a vitally important fact—a highly successful and influential father who could not come to grips with an undisciplined son who flirted with failure in numerous directions. The father reached great heights of power. What would become of the son?

The second dimension, aside from the glue of the family, is the social reality of intense academic competition. Everything that defines an individual and his or her future is shaped by his or her performance in school. Every student wants to stand first in his or her class. It is not enough to do well. You must be at the top of your class or close to it. Intellect is worshiped.

When I was in school, every student's grades and position in the class were printed in the leading newspapers for all to see. Success or failure was reason for public pride or shame. One of my closest friends toyed with suicide after his high-school exams because he did not stand first in the entire city of New Delhi. Another one of my classmates in college actually burned himself to death because he did not make the grade.

Such distortion that has hurt so many still pervades many cultures. It is plainly wrong, but it is cherished with a passion.

This combination of the standard at home and the standard in society became a volatile mix in my life. I showed early signs that I would not be the boast of a powerful dad. This was not deliberate; it was just either the lack of capacity or capacity in search of a purpose. Life crept along while the long arm of cultural pressure was gradually creeping up on me, and I knew I would not pass the test.

Every morning, we would awaken to men and women standing outside our home, waiting for just one minute of my father's time. He held the keys to numerous jobs and contacts. With folded hands, they would plead for a chance at a job. On his way to the car, he would nod to them as if to say, "Leave it with me." And the truth is that many were helped by his connections. Scores of people revered his name because of such power. Could I not also have benefited someday from his influence? But too much lurked behind the scenes to offer a simplistic explanation.

In addition, my father had a foreboding side. With his enormous position in life, he battled a volatile temper. My lack of focus made it a situation awaiting crisis. That combination was to bring him and me into a relationship that I now regret. I am ever grateful to God that it did not end the way it began.

As committed as he was to a brilliant career for me, I was just as desirous of living for the sports field—a love of my life in which he had no interest. He had a point. Every boy growing up wanted to become a cricketer and play for India, just as every youngster in New York wants to play for the Yankees. But I did show some promise. I played for many teams at my college—cricket, hockey, tennis, and table tennis—yet never once did my dad come to see me play, even in any big game. We were marching to different drumbeats.

Throughout these years, I never lost respect for him. To this day, I believe my father was a good man, indeed, even a great man, but he did not know how to get close to a hurting, struggling child. I, for my part, pondered within and lived with my own private pain. Over the years I have come to believe that these things matter more than ordinary people may realize, but perhaps less than extremists would lead us to believe. Somehow we learn to cope, except that it places us near the edge of self-rejection and renders us more vulnerable when dreams are shattered.

Let me illustrate this point.

A few years ago, a former Olympic athlete came to visit me. He was looking for some direction in his life. He was a strong and solidly built man. It was a privilege to be around him—just in the hopes that muscles were contagious!

He told me of the time he was representing his country at the Olympics. It was a story of dreams that had struggled against a potential nightmare. From the age of twelve, the Olympics had been all he labored for. He had put every penny he earned and every purchase he made into someday becoming a gold medalist in the event he loved. He was totally focused. This is what he wanted. But he had a very turbulent relationship with his father, who had no interest in this dream of his, and, therefore, he had funded every penny himself.

When he was only seventeen, he filmed the world champion in the event for which he was training and broke down his every stride, frame by frame, to study his technique. He then had himself filmed in the same distance and matched it, stride for stride. By precisely piecing together where he was losing the precious seconds to the world champion, he determined to bridge the gap. Through sheer willpower, discipline, and courage, his goal was within reach.

He made the cut for his country's team, and life was suddenly like being atop a floating cloud. He won every heat and was emerging as the surprise and potential winner when the finals came. Was this a dream or was it real? No, it was real, he reminded himself.

He was at the starting point for the finals, and his nation was watching. Millions were cheering for him, and hearts were racing, expecting this "country-boy-makes-it-big" story to hit the headlines the next day. In fact, I remember watching the event. The gun was about to go off, signaling the start. This was the moment he had waited for most of his life. But the mind with all its tenacity and resoluteness is also a storehouse of unuttered yearnings.

"From out of nowhere," he said, "an unexpected thought suddenly flooded my mind—*I wonder if my father is watching me.*"

That unanticipated thought momentarily overcame him and may have added a fraction of a second to his first two strides, robbing him of the gold. With great credit, he still won the bronze. The third fastest in the world is no mean accomplishment. Yet, to him, the victory on the track lost its luster when measured against the deeper yearnings of life—the approval of the ones you love. Little did this Olympian know how my heart was beating as he shared this story with me. I understood him well.

Young dreams may be wild ones, but they are never corrected by ridiculing them. They must be steered by a loving voice that has earned the right to be heard, not one enforced by means of power. This is a very difficult lesson for parents to learn. And as cultures lose their restraining power, there will be greater need for mutual love and respect between parents and children if a relationship of trust is to be built, rather than banking on authority because of position.

Probably the most wrenching words I ever heard my father say to me were, "You will never make anything of your life!" And frankly, it seemed he was right. He was trying only to jolt me into reality. My mother's comfort could only carry me so far. In that sense, that fateful day when I cycled home was a critical point at which we ought to have sat down and talked. But I suppose the freedom to talk does not emerge in a vacuum. The moment of opportunity is built on hours of preparation.

WHERE DO I SEEK THAT I MIGHT FIND?

Our strained relationship was only made worse by a foundational, self-perpetuating thought. If life had no purpose, why try to work it out anyway? When I talk about purpose and meaning, I do not just mean some sense of existential peace. I mean a direction to life that upholds both reason and emotion. This is very critical to understand.

Now as I have moved to the West, I find that although many young people here identify with the problem, it is unexplainably ignored in the adult world. Why do I say this?

In the corporate world, every major company formulates a mission statement. That, in turn, is invoked when measuring achievements and failures. If a company does not know why it exists, then it will never know if it is failing or succeeding. How indicting, then, it is to all of us who will labor for hours to establish a mission statement for a company to sell toothpicks or tombstones but never pause long enough to write one out for our individual lives.

At the very point of writing, I have read an article interviewing one of Australia's great cricketers. He is in the midst of the world cup of cricket, representing his country. Rather teary in his otherwise "no-holds-barred" posture to life, he muttered a regret. Even as he is playing these matches, his wife is minutes away from delivering their second child, thousands of miles away. "I was gone for the first one and now am absent for the second. I have concluded that cricket is important to my life, but it isn't everything."

But that invokes a question, does it not? What is everything? Is anything everything? Why are we so eager to prove to the world that we are the best at what we do and care not for why or who we are?

How I wish there had been answers for me to such questions. Maybe there were, but I could not discern them amid the deluge of voices in a religious land. Purpose is to life what the skeleton is to the body. The muscle may have strength, but it needs support and attachment. All my pursuits had no supporting structure. Life drifted with affections and sports, but without ultimate purpose.

Just think of the alternatives our cultures have given to us. Pleasure, wealth, power, fame, fate, charity, peace, education, ethnicity—the list goes on endlessly. And when none of these work, some amalgam of spirituality and pragmatism is embraced. But these pursuits do not tell us why we are here in the first place. These may be ways of ordering one's life, but is life to be defined by what I pursue, or must my pursuit be defined by what life was meant to be?

In a culture where the academic is the ultimate and my life was not measuring up, a culture where philosophy is abundant but purpose is never imparted, where could I turn? The ultimate loss is the loss of face when failure attends. This thing we call shame is deeply embedded in the Hindi language, so much so that when one fails, part of the scolding is to be branded a shameless individual. That night it seemed as if I had lost face forever, and my punishment was both a metaphor and a reality.

THE SEEKER FINDS OUT HE IS SOUGHT

Somewhere in the midst of all this turmoil, the Hound of Heaven was on my trail. His footprints are everywhere as I look over my shoulder now. He was, indeed, nearer than I thought. I can see now, in hindsight, the trail that is evident, even in the grimmest moments. When you live in a small, two-bedroom home with four siblings and two parents, you cannot run for a hiding place. Yet it is utterly amazing how one can hide within oneself.

But the work of God had long begun. From out of the blue, one day my sister was invited to a youth event that would feature music and a speaker. She invited me to attend this meeting with her. On this occasion the visiting speaker was a man who, though a total stranger to me, was a well-respected Christian leader internationally.[3] My memory of it is too blurred to recall exactly all that transpired. But this I know. He spoke on a text that is probably the best-known text in the Bible: "For God so loved the world, that he gave his only begotten Son, that whosoever believeth in him should not perish, but have everlasting life" (John 3:16 KJV).

Even more powerful than what he said was his demeanor, and his heart came through in his words. There were both tenderness and power. Unaccustomed to being at such an event, I found myself walking conspicuously alone to the front at his invitation to trust in Jesus Christ as my Lord and my Savior. Although I had been raised in a church, I held out such little hope that its message had anything to do with life that I grasped only a portion of what he said. None of these things meant anything to me. To this vocabulary I was a stranger. I only knew that my life was wrong and that I needed somebody to make it right. I wanted new hungers, new longings, new disciplines, and new loves. I knew God had to matter. I just did not know how to find Him.

I left that night with a hint in my mind that there was something so right about the message, even though I had not got it all together. My confusion notwithstanding, a very important context was put into place. As the weeks went by, I continued to attend all of the popular Hindu festivals and to enjoy watching dramatic presentations of their mythology. I had an ardent Hindu friend who worked very hard at getting me to embrace the Hindu view of life.

Then a very significant event took place. I was cycling past a cremation site and stopped to ask the Hindu priest where that person, whose body was nothing more than a pile of ashes, was now.

"Young man," he said, "that is a question you will be asking all your life, and you will never find a certain answer."

If that is the best a priest can do, I thought, *what hope is there for a novice like me?*

As the months went by, without the further explanation that I needed, the continued loss of meaning led me to a tragic moment. Had I read the atheistic philosopher Jean Paul Sartre at that stage of my life, he would have confirmed every sense of isolation that I felt. Two of his best-selling books, *Nausea* and *No Exit*, exactly described my state. Sartre went so far as to say that the only question he could not answer was why he did not commit suicide. Is it not amazing that when life seems meaningless, the poets and artists are unafraid to plead guilty while the rationalists denounce that posture and wax eloquent with little reason?

My decision was firm but calm. A quiet exit would save my family and me any further failure. I put my plan into action. As a result, I found myself on a hospital bed, having been rushed there in the throes of an attempted suicide. In that hospital room, a Bible was brought to me, and in the desolation of my condition, a passage of Scripture was read to me. The speaker's message from that youth event still rang in my ears. I needed it as a base on which to build. He had preached from the third chapter of the Gospel according to John about God's love. Now in the hospital, I was being read the fourteenth chapter of John about God's purpose.

The words in that chapter were spoken to the apostle Thomas, who, as I said, came to India. His memorial exists to this day, just a few miles away from where I was born. Remember that Jesus had said to him, "I am the way and the truth and the life. No man comes to the Father except through Me." But my attention was captured by a few words farther along, when Jesus said to His disciples, "Because I live, you shall live also." Again, I was not sure of all that it meant. I knew it meant more than just biological life. Piecing together God's love in Christ, the way that was provided because of Christ, and the promise of life through Him, on that hospital bed I made my commitment to give my life and my pursuits into His hands. The struggles of my relationships, my origin, and my destiny were all addressed in that conversation Jesus had with His disciples two thousand years ago. My commitment stands now as the most wonderful transaction I ever made. I turned my life completely over to Jesus Christ.

In the same poem I quoted earlier, Oscar Wilde said:

And all the woe that moved him so
That gave that bitter cry,
And the wild regrets and bloody sweats,
None knew so well as I:
For he who lives more lives than one
More deaths than one must die . . .
And every human heart that breaks
In prison-cell or yard,
Is as that broken box that gave
Its treasure to the Lord,
And filled the unclean leper's house
With the scent of costliest nard.
Ah! Happy day they whose hearts can break
And peace and pardon win!
How else may man make straight his plan
And cleanse his soul from Sin?
How else but through a broken heart
May Lord Christ enter in?

I walked out of that hospital room a new man. The Lord Christ had entered in. The transformation was as dramatic as I could have ever imagined. There is no other way to describe it. From then on, my longings, my hopes, my dreams, and my every effort has been to live for Him who rescued me, to study for Him who gave me this mind, to serve Him who fashioned my will, and to speak for Him who gave me a voice.

The passion for learning, the recognition of the value of study, and the need to understand great thinkers and their thoughts—all were gradually put into their legitimate place. Our intellect is not intended to be an end in itself, but only a means to the very mind of God. Books, which were once a curse, became a gold mine.

The Hebrews had a motif by which they symbolized the ideal: "Every man under his own fig tree." If the Lord were to allow me a metaphor today, it would be, "Every man in his own library." The very pursuits that at one time brought so much inner heartache are now for me the transcending delight of my heart. Little did I know the long academic journey that lay ahead of me. I have loved it.

So much has transpired since that day that it would fill volumes. God has given me the privilege of speaking for Him on every continent and in dozens of cities, presenting a defense of the Christian faith in some of the finest institutions of the world. I am privileged beyond measure. I am as much at home in New Delhi as I am in Atlanta or Toronto. I love the peoples of this world, each with their accents and cuisines and idiosyncrasies. I have truly enjoyed the challenge and privilege that being a Christian apologist has brought my way. Christian apologetics is the task of presenting a defense of the person and the message of Jesus Christ. Over the years, I have become more convinced than ever that He is exactly who He claimed to be—God incarnate, who came to give us life to the fullest and to point us to the beauty and freedom of truth. The thrill of seeing thousands of lives transformed is a thrill I cannot deny.

The Pattern Unfolds

As I bring this chapter to a close, I would like to share how a purposeful design emerges when God weaves a pattern from what, to us, may often seem disparate threads.

Some years ago, I was visiting a place where some of the most beautiful saris are made. The sari, of course, is the garment worn by Indian women. It is usually about six yards long. Wedding saris are a work of art; they are rich in gold and silver threads, resplendent with an array of colors.

The place I was visiting was known for making the best wedding saris in the world. I expected to see some elaborate system of machines and designs that would boggle the mind. Not so! Each sari was being made individually by a father-and-son team. The father sat above on a platform two to three feet higher than the son, surrounded by several spools of thread, some dark, some shining. The son did just one thing. At a nod from his father, he would move the shuttle from one side to the other and back again. The father would gather some threads in his fingers, nod once more, and the son would move the shuttle again. This would be repeated for hundreds of hours, till you would begin to see a magnificent pattern emerging.

The son had the easy task—just to move at the father's nod. All along, the father had the design in his mind and brought the right threads together.

The more I reflect on my own life and study the lives of others, I am fascinated to see the design God has for each one of us, individually, if we would only respond to Him. Little reminders come my way to show the threads He has woven into this life. The following story is a small pointer to that end.

Almost thirty years to the day after my surrender to Christ, my wife and I were visiting India and decided to visit my grandmother's grave. I had only vague recollections of her funeral, the first funeral I had ever attended. I had a challenge trying to tell the cemetery manager the year of her death. We finally arrived at the year—as I recalled I was probably nine or ten when it might have happened. After thumbing through old registers that were bigger than his desk, we eventually found her name. With the help of a gardener, we walked through the accumulated weeds and dirt and rubble in the cemetery until we found the large slab of stone marking her grave.

No one had visited her grave for almost thirty years. With his little bucket of water and a small brush, the gardener cleared off the caked-on dirt and, to our utter surprise, under her name, a verse gradually appeared. My wife clasped my hand and said, "Look at the verse!" It read, "Because I live, you shall live also." As I said, He was on my trail long before I knew it.

As the years have gone by, we have made a study of when the gospel first made inroads into our family. On both my mother's and my father's sides, five and six generations ago, the first believers came from the highest caste of the Hindu priesthood. The first to come to the Lord was a woman. She was intrigued by the message brought to her village by missionaries and continued to seek them out, in spite of her family's terrible displeasure. But one day, as she was about to leave the missionary compound in order to be home before her family found out where she had been, the doors of the compound were shut because a cholera epidemic had broken out in the village. She had to remain with the missionaries for several weeks until the time of quarantine was past. By that time, she had committed her life to the Lord. The walls of a closed compound were the means of bringing her face to face with Jesus Christ.

All walls are not barriers. They may be there for a purpose. As I look back upon the journey, there is one image and two poets who come to mind. In the New Testament, we are told of the conversion of Saul of Tarsus. He, of course, was a terrorist to the Christians. God graciously tracked him down with His love to make him one of His choice apostles. Those who were once his friends now threatened his life. The disciples put him in a basket and lowered him over a city wall that he might escape his tormentors.

For me, the torment was within. God planted the feet of some who lifted me in a basket of love and persuasion and lowered me over the walls I could not scale on my own. Such is the grace of Christ who meets us where we are.

Readers of English poetry will recall the turbulent life of Francis Thompson. His father longed for him to study at Oxford, but Francis lost his way in drugs and failed to make the grade on more than one occasion. Those who knew him knew that inside was a slumbering genius, if only his life could be rescued.

When Francis Thompson finally succumbed to the pursuing Christ, he penned his immortal "Hound of Heaven," describing the years behind the moment of transaction:

> I fled Him down the nights and down the days.
> I fled Him down the arches of the years,
> I fled Him down the labyrinthine ways
> of my own mind: And in the mist of tears
> I hid from Him, and under running laughter
> Up vistaed hopes I sped;
> Down titanic glooms of chasmed fears
> From those strong feet that followed, that followed after
> For though I knew His love that followed
> Yet I was sore adread
> Lest having Him I have naught else beside.

All that I took from thee I did but take

Not for thy harms

But just that thou might'st seek it in my arms.

All which thy child's mistake fancies are lost

I have stored for thee at home:

"Rise, clasp my hand, and come."

Halts by me that footfall:

is my gloom after all,

shade of His hand, outstretched caressingly.

Ah, fondest, blindest, weakest,

I am he whom thou seekest!

Thou dravest love from thee, that dravest me.

What a wonderful day it was when I stopped running and, by His strength, let the embrace of His love envelop me. The words of a famous hymn by Charles Wesley reflect that triumph and my story:

Long my imprisoned spirit lay,

Fast bound in sin and nature's night.

Thine eye diffused a quickening ray,

I woke, the dungeon flamed with light.

My chains fell off, my heart was free,

I rose, went forth and followed thee.[4]

Only one thing need be added. I was twenty years old when my family moved to Canada. There, my mom and dad made their commitments to Christ too. It was a new day for all of us. My dad worked hard at recovering the lost years. In 1974, I was in my twenties, young in the ministry, and I was in Cambodia, preaching in some very fearsome circumstances. My father sent a letter with me that he wanted me to read after I left. In it he reflected upon the days when all seemed lost to me and to him in our relationship. It was a beautiful letter. I read it, lying in my bed in Phnom Penh.

One line summed it up when he said, "I thank God that He considered our family in calling as one of His servants, one of my children."

He passed away in 1979 at the age of sixty-seven. I do miss him in these wonderful years of ministry. He would have been such an encouragement. God's grace is beyond description. He lifted all of us over the walls of our own imprisonment.

So much for the story. Now to the argument.

Chapter Two

ADDRESSING A HEAVENLY HOME

ONE OF THE GREATEST OPPORTUNITIES EVER ACCORDED A MEMBER of our family took place when Queen Elizabeth and Prince Philip visited India in the late fifties.

My younger brother, who happened to be seven or eight years old and the youngest member of the choir at the Delhi Cathedral, was to be formally introduced to the queen following a Sunday service. He certainly never lacked for counsel on how to prepare for this extraordinary meeting. We ceaselessly coached him, repeatedly reminding him to address her as "Your Majesty" and not "Auntie," the latter being a typical way of showing respect in India. The moment came, and he passed with flying colors.

Unknown to us, his meeting with the queen was carried on television back in England as part of a news clip, prompting calls to the television station to inquire whether "that cute little boy" was available for adoption. Since that day, at any hint of his misbehavior, we siblings have never missed the opportunity to suggest that we should have taken the English up on their offer! Four decades have gone by since that wonderful memory of bowing before the queen, and he never misses the opportunity to remind us of his greater privilege.

Meeting historic figures is not a humdrum experience. Lines are rehearsed, questions are debated, and protocol is practiced long before the event. I have no doubt that the more elaborate the pomp and pageantry accompanying the occasion, the greater the fear of saying or doing something improper.

One can only imagine a conversation in the home of Andrew and Simon Peter, the earliest followers of Jesus, when Andrew first informed their family that he believed he had met the long-awaited Messiah. This redeemer figure was the only hope for a nation languishing under the scourge of successive foreign rulers. Any good Israelite had prayed for the coming of the One who would free His people. A cynic at the evening meal probably choked on his food when the announcement was made by Andrew that he and Simon had just come back from meeting the prophesied deliverer. Many barbs were probably withstood while the brothers insisted they were not out of their minds. They had talked to Him, spent hours with Him, and Andrew had even been given the opportunity to ask Him any question he desired.

Out of sheer curiosity, one at the table may have muttered, "And what, perchance, did you ask Him?"

"I asked Him where He lived," came the confident reply.

Can we not hear it? Silence around the table.

"That was the best you could do, Andrew? To ask Him *where He lived*?"

Could there not have been a better question that would have put Jesus' claim to the test? At least that is how we, in our time, might have remonstrated. Why did Andrew, face to face with Him who claimed such unique status, not pose a greater challenge than a simple query, "Where do You live?" Malcolm Muggeridge, the English journalist, remarks in his autobiography on the opportunities he had to interview noted dignitaries around the world. Being an incurable cynic and iconoclast, and just for the sake of playing to the readership, he would ask a deliberately absurd and belittling question, for example, asking a bishop, at a most poignant moment and before a highly reverential audience, "Are bishops really necessary?" He did that, he conceded, because he leveraged his profession as a journalist to live off shock value, at the cost of substance.

Was this some kind of "shock" question, a trivializing gibe from Andrew so that they could find out the street address of the Messiah and then heap scorn upon the claimant? Was he playing to the audience too? The more I have thought of it, the more I am convinced that the would-be disciple had sound reasons for asking what he did. His serious investigation into the person of Jesus had begun. Was this truly the Christ, the Anointed One? For nearly two thousand years, the prophets had told of His coming. Was this that fulfillment? Let us take a hard look at what prompted so basic a question for so monumental a claim.

A PROVOCATIVE INTRODUCTION

The setting of the disciple's question is given to us in John's Gospel, the first chapter. Immediately one is struck by the casualness with which Jesus made His entry. There is no drumbeat, no great tumult, no parade to herald the One whose name was to be on the lips of humanity in a way no other name had ever been. There was no time given for rehearsals.

John the Baptizer was given the honor of making the unadorned announcement. John, draped in strange attire and living off even stranger food, was gaining a huge following. In the eyes of the devout, he was a prophet of supreme honor. And in truth, before his birth, the angel had spoken of his privileged and purposeful God-given calling. His assigned place in history was to be the one who introduced Jesus to the world. Of all the fanfare that he could have mustered for his declaration, he chose instead a simple utterance. This was so bereft of regal accompaniment that no "king-maker" would have conceived such modesty for so world-changing an announcement. And especially not in the East.

Yet, on a given day and at a divinely appointed moment, Jesus came to John to be baptized. Awe-stricken by this privilege, John stuttered out his own unworthiness of such an honor, declaring that he was not even fit to untie the shoes of his Lord. How could he dare to baptize Him? The scene is memorialized to this day by the dove that descended upon Jesus. As this heavenly affirmation was given, John looked at two of his own disciples and said, "Look, the Lamb of God."

It is hard to resist the sobering portent behind the designation. The average Jewish family grew up with lambs and sacrifices. The temple probably reeked of animals and their slaughter, especially on the Day of Atonement. The exterior grandeur of the temple housed only a rather grim and messy-looking altar. Every lamb sacrificed was from the possessions of the petitioner and was thus, a lamb of men offered to God. In fact, it was not even a representative from *among* men, an equal. It was a lamb *owned* by men, a dumb, unsuspecting animal brought into the temple, never to return.

Now, in this appointed moment in history, an offering came from God Himself and was given *by* God on behalf of humanity. This was the Lamb of God. But how could such a thing be? One born for the designed purpose of being sacrificed on the altar someday? Would not that have provoked a different question from those wanting to become His disciples, especially since that was the jolting introduction chosen by John?

Someone well versed in the Scriptures would have probably harked back immediately to the narrative in Genesis 22, in which Abraham was called upon to offer up his long-awaited son, Isaac. As father and son walked toward the mountain, Isaac asked the obvious question, "The fire and the wood are here, but where is the lamb?" As the story unfolds, Isaac himself was laid upon the altar and readied as a sacrifice.

At the last moment, as Abraham's hand holding the blade descended upon Isaac, God exclaimed, "Stop! There is another I will provide." God, who had planned this all along to test Abraham, providentially trapped a ram in the thicket to serve as a substitute for Isaac, even as it represented a different lamb that would come on a different day.

John's announcement, in effect, said, "Here He is—the Lamb of God who was promised long ago." The day was approaching when there would be another hill and another altar, and this time the hand of the Father would not stop the slaying.

The disciples of John who heard his pronouncement of Jesus as the Lamb of God turned from him to follow Jesus. The first question Jesus put to them had deliberate and reasoned bluntness: "What do you want?" They had no real understanding at this point that they were following One who was on a one-way journey that would ultimately end at an altar.

I wonder if any of us would have asked what they did in that momentous encounter. A better question might have been, "What does John mean when he calls You the Lamb of God? Are You headed for a gruesome end?" Instead, they were interested in His beginnings, asking the astounding question, "Where do You live?" I made the assertion earlier that in the East, the home is the defining cultural indicator. Everything that determines who you are and what your future bodes is tied into your heritage and your social standing. Absolutely everything.

The first time I returned to speak in India after an eleven-year absence, my wife (who is from Canada) witnessed firsthand the esteem conferred by one's family. At a reception that was held in our honor in Bombay at which I was to speak, her astonishment lay in the way I was introduced. The very long and formal introduction I was given was filled with superlatives. Yet, in its entirety, absolutely nothing was said about me. Instead, it was a lavish description of my father's credentials and accomplishments. It was one of those moments when you wanted to look around and identify this highly decorated individual. Then the last line was tagged on—"and this is his son, who is to speak to us." That was the only line that referred to me.

My immediate response was to laugh on the inside. But it suddenly dawned on me that I was representing somebody bigger than myself—my father. Because of him, I was given a hearing. I knew I was in the East. An introduction in the West, particularly in North America, is all about what *I* have or have not accomplished. The credentials are individual, almost as if an individual owes even his beginning to himself. There is little or no mention of family. But in India, the country of my father's birth, my father's credentials, my mother's birth, and my roots become very important to the audience.

I notice this significant difference to this very day. In the West, it does not take long for a stranger to ask, "Where do you work?" or "What is your business?" The questioner's thoughts are forming a picture, to determine your financial profile and corporate influence so that the conversation can follow that trail. In the East, the question comes with equal deliberateness, "Which was your home city when you lived here?" "Which part of town did you live in?" "What did your father do?" Names, addresses, and family background are very defining. East or West, the goal may be the same, to place you in society's assigned place. Only the routing is different.

You see, in a stratified society, your home address gives the inquirer literally a wealth of information about you. The privilege of birth opens doors. It is not at all surprising that Nathanael's response when he was first told about Jesus was, "Can anything good come out of Nazareth?" That is followed some verses later by, "Is this not the son of Joseph, the carpenter?" How in the name of reason could the answer to the hopes and dreams of Israel, in search of the Messiah, come from a city of such low esteem and from a family of such modest professional status? The best way for them to find out whether He could really be who John described Him to be was to follow Him to His house—to the earthly address of the One who claimed to be the Son of God.

Jesus' answer builds the intrigue. He did not give a street name or a house's identification. He simply said, "Come and see." They went with Him to see where He was staying and evidently spent the night there. Andrew returned to tell his brother Simon that they had found the Messiah, that is, the Christ, and invited him to come and see also.

The next day, Philip, who was also from the same city, invited Nathanael to join them by saying, "We have found the one Moses wrote about in the Law, and about whom the prophets also wrote—Jesus of Nazareth, the son of Joseph." There you have it—the city and the parentage. Nathanael is predictably cynical and is given the same challenge: "Come and see."

A MEMORABLE ENCOUNTER

The Scriptures remain silent on numerous issues. Matters in which we would be greatly interested are left without description. What kind of home did Jesus live in? What kind of carpentry did He do, if any? How was His home furnished? What wealth or poverty did it bespeak? I have often thought that instead of the space given to ponderous genealogies, some other details of Jesus' life would have been of greater interest to the reader. How much did He earn? What kind of clothes did He wear? What did He look like?

But maybe this is where God's vision of reality seeks to lift us from the enslavement and distortion of our earth-driven view. Historic figures have homes to visit for posterity; the Lord of history left no home. Luminaries leave libraries and write their memoirs; He left one book, penned by ordinary people. Deliverers speak of winning through might and conquest; He spoke of a place in the heart.

Would it have been that difficult to preserve an article of clothing or a piece of furniture, just so we could put it in a museum for the world to see? One can go into little towns today and see excavations of homes from Jesus' time. Why was not His own home preserved? In a museum in Turkey, one can see the sword of Mohammed and what are claimed to be strands from his beard. Recently we have been informed that a tooth of Gautama, the Buddha, has been found. We can go back across time and see extraordinary collections of artifacts connected to monarchs and heroes from even before the time of Christ.

He who owns the cattle on a thousand hills left no such information. Of Christ we are told that He did not have a place to lay His head. The same Gospel writer forthrightly states this: "In the beginning was the Word, and the Word was with God, and the Word was God. . . . [And] the Word became flesh and made his dwelling among us" (John 1:1, 14). John's "In the beginning" has a striking parallel with the first words of the Scriptures, "In the beginning God. . . ."

As important as His earthly parentage was, His home address was not an earthly one—for in a very real sense, He had no beginning. Amid the "where" and "when" questions that plague our finitude, there is no such encumbrance for the eternal and infinite One. To lift them beyond the here and now was the task ahead of Jesus when He said to them, "Come and see." I suspect there were going to be shock and a need of much explanation. Andrew had a reason for asking the question, and Jesus was offering a journey of thought as His answer. We will take that journey. At this point, put yourself in Andrew's sandals. He had been invited to the home of the One identified by a recognized prophet as the Lamb of God. Andrew went. What was he anticipating? Would he be disappointed?

Billy Graham tells of the time he was at a crusade in Pittsburgh. He had just entered the hotel lobby where he was staying for the week and, with a couple of his teammates, walked into the elevator where a handful of businessmen were in conversation. As the elevator began to lift, one of the businessmen said, "I hear Billy Graham is in this hotel." One of the others who recognized Dr. Graham smiled, looked at the one who had made the comment, pointed to Billy Graham, and said, "That's he." The startled businessman paused, looked again at Billy Graham, and said, "What an anticlimax!" Being the humble man that he is, Dr. Graham fully sympathized with the person's disappointment and admitted that this was all there was to him.

What was this man really expecting? Some haloed and winged figure who did not need an elevator and who would only be seen praying and rising on air? In our human imagination, we so often perceive our heroes to be something larger than life. We exalt them in ways that do them disservice. We make them to be almost plastic in our imaginations. And when they bleed or grow old or stumble, we either cast them aside or find some way to perpetuate the myth. To sustain this illusion in our minds, we build statues and erect monuments, and artists paint them with haloes to establish their surreal personae. We convince ourselves that they are or were something essentially different from the rest of us.

This one time in history this person *was* essentially different from all of us. But, from Nazareth? The son of a carpenter? Even the temple that was erected as God's dwelling place had beauty and wealth expended beyond imagination. Now that God had come in the flesh, His home was so paltry by comparison. To help sort it out, Nathanael is brought into the picture. He was one of those who was so committed to the truth that when he was invited to come and meet Jesus, he agreed to go along, probably in the hope of dispelling this "deception" that had been manufactured in the minds of his friends. But when he came within range of Jesus' voice, Jesus spoke those carefully chosen words: "Here is a true Israelite, in whom there is nothing false."

There lay the first surprise. There are few things as disquieting to a person as having his or her inner thoughts laid bare by the words of a stranger.

He had come to "check out" this person and instead, his own character was revealed for what it really was. "How do You know me?" demanded Nathanael. And Jesus replied, "I saw you under the fig tree, before Philip called you."

What did this mean to Nathanael?

Was he pondering something when under the fig tree? Did he have a premonition while under that tree that a life-defining moment was around the corner? Was it a private moment of which he thought no one else was aware? Something in Jesus' disclosure made Nathanael react impulsively, almost rashly, and he uttered these life-changing words: "Rabbi, you are the Son of God; you are the King of Israel" (John 1:49). I believe Jesus jarred Nathanael's skepticism by a gentle uncovering of the thoughts and intents of Nathanael's own heart.

It was at this very point that Andrew's question—"Where do You live?"—met a most incredible answer. Jesus had seen Nathanael when Nathanael did not know he was being watched. He identified the determination with which Nathanael pursued reality, which certainly gained his attention. In one of his psalms, King David confessed that he could not flee from God's presence, for God knew him in his inmost being—"Wherever I go, You are there" (see Ps. 139:7–10). Nathanael had just realized the same truth.

Jesus also knew that Nathanael did not think very much of Nazareth. Recognizing what was in his heart, Jesus challenged his impulsive declaration and said, "You believe because I told you I saw you under the fig tree. You shall see greater things than that. . . . I tell you the truth, you shall see heaven open, and the angels of God ascending and descending on the Son of Man" (John 1:50–51).

Jesus, in short, said, "You are shocked because I revealed you to yourself? Wait until you see the full disclosure of who I am and from whence I come." He took Nathanael from explaining the puzzlement of lesser things to a destination of glorious insights.

The description He gave of angels ascending and descending on the Son of Man was not tossed out in a vacuum. It pointed to Jesus' "parentage." Peter, Andrew, and Nathanael all knew the story of the father of their nation, Jacob, which really provided the backdrop for Jesus' answer.

The Old Testament carefully records that incident. As a young man, Jacob had cheated his brother, Esau, and was on the run to flee from his wrath. On his journey to distant parts, he thought he was alone, far from the eye of anyone else. He had been raised in a home in which the altar, as the center of the family's worship of God, played a significant part. His grandfather, Abraham, was known as "the man of the tent and the man of the altar." Abraham saw his home as temporary but his worship as permanent. Now, on the run, Jacob was homeless and altarless. When he reached a place called Luz, he slept with a stone for a pillow. Even for a desert dweller, that was rough.

And while he slept, the Lord came to him in a dream in which he saw a stairway that reached from the earth to heaven. Angels ascended and descended the stairway. And there above it stood the Lord, who said, "I am the LORD, the God of your father Abraham and the God of Isaac" (Gen. 28:13). When Jacob awoke from his sleep, he thought to himself, "Surely the LORD is in this place, and I was not aware of it. . . . How awesome is this place! This is none other than the house of God; this is the gate of heaven" (vv. 16–17). Jacob took the stone pillow and left it as a marker in the place he was now going to call Bethel—meaning, "the house of God."

Whether the disciples fully understood it or not, a thundering message was given when Jesus spoke those words to Nathanael. He staked a claim. Were they aware that the Lord who fashioned the heavens and the earth was standing beside them? Angelic hosts attended His abode. Even at that, we struggle to word it precisely. The word *abode* immediately brings to mind the concepts of residing and of boundaries, neither of which is a fitting term for One who is without beginning and is omnipresent. Jacob found out that God's presence to bless could transform any location into the house of God. Now the disciples learned the same. They were inclined to judge Jesus by His earthly father, Joseph the carpenter. They were trying to measure His worth by His earthly home, Nazareth. He opened up to them the truth that any earthly setting at which He is present becomes the gateway to heaven. What comfort this must have brought them.

But, more than that, they rightly inferred from what Jesus said that He had come from His heavenly Father, who was the God of Abraham, Isaac, and Jacob. He took them farther back than their own understanding and lifted them to further heights to show them that the word *home* was at best only an analogical representation of living with God. The disciples were clearly overwhelmed by that initial impact. They did not fully comprehend all that this encounter was going to mean to them. Their lives would change beyond their wildest dreams, so that the day would come when they would leave their own homes to tell the world of Jesus of Nazareth. "If you marvel at what I have shown you of yourself, Nathanael, this is only the beginning of what awaits you when I disclose My glory to you." *That*, He assured them, would be no anticlimax.

GLIMPSES OF ANOTHER HOME

Jesus broached some very significant truths in this simple interaction—truths that lift our thoughts to the limit emerge from this first conversation. Let us engage these thoughts one at a time.

The primary and unique indicator here, literally and figuratively, is Jesus' revelation of the realm of His existence. To ask for the "where" of Jesus' home is the same as asking the "when" of God's beginning. Such categories are necessary in our finite existence, because there was a time when we were not. But God transcends such categories. Jesus' references to a heavenly dwelling and to the angels ascending and descending in His service point to the fact that He is the Lord of heaven and earth who exists eternally and necessarily. His existence precedes every spatial metaphor. Just as it is impossible for Him not to be, so it is not necessary for Him to have a *place* to live. That is precisely what He said to David, who wanted to build a temple where God could "dwell" (2 Sam. 7:5). It is more sensible to ask where He has promised to *bless* us than to ask where His locus of existence is.

Such transcending categories seem so beyond our reach, and yet they intimate our ultimate destiny. Even now, we realize that concepts such as time, space, and motion are so bound up into the limited dimensions of our understanding of the nature of reality that for most of us, they seem the domain of geniuses. Yet the deeper we penetrate into such mysteries, the more inexorably we are drawn to the lowest common denominator of what makes life the way it is. We look for the minutest part of reality in the physical world so that we can, in the words of the scientist, arrive at a theory of everything.

Jesus reversed the process. He told us that the only way we could understand who we are is to cast our gaze not on the equation that binds it all together, but on the relationship toward which we move in the sum total of our being. It is the assemblage of an object that gives it its, not the reduction of it. In the words of Jesus to Nathanael, our amazement will know no bounds when we understand all that the realm of God's existence means.

No other claimant to divine or prophetic status would ever have answered this question of his home in this manner. Even John the Baptizer took great pains to remind his followers of this difference: "A man can receive only what is given him from heaven. . . . The one who comes from above is above all; the one who is from the earth belongs to the earth, and speaks as one from the earth. The one who comes from heaven is above all. He testifies to what He has seen and heard" (John 3:27, 31–32).

Even if they are teaching truth, all others who have claimed or been accorded prophetic status are still at best human beings on whom this call from God was bestowed. Their assignment is a given one; they are the human receptors. Jesus, in distinction, is the Supreme Giver Himself. He is "from above," say the Gospel writers.

In another conversation, Jesus stated that His ascent into heaven was preceded by His descent from heaven (see John 3:13). Implicit in that claim is the assertion that His knowledge of everything is perfect and complete. That alone sets Him apart. His vision of reality, His explanation of life, His opening up of mysteries, and His glimpses into what matters and what does not matter proceed out of His being in the eternal. And that is the point. His earthly sojourn was not an origination, but a visitation.

Every other person who is at the heart of any religion has had his or her *beginning* either in fancy or in fact. But nevertheless, there is a beginning. Jesus' birth in Bethlehem was a moment preceded by eternity. His being neither originated in time nor came about by the will of humanity. The Author of time, who lived in the eternal, was made incarnate in time that we might live with the eternal in view. In that sense, the message of Christ was not the introduction of a religion, but an introduction to truth about reality as God alone knows it. To deny Jesus' message while pursuing spirituality is to conjure an imaginary religion in an attempt to see heaven while sight is confined to the earth. That is precisely what Jesus challenged when He said, "I have come that [you] may have life" (John 10:10). His life spells living. Your life or my life, apart from Him, spells death.

POSITIONED BY TRANSCENDENCE

"Where do You live?" asked the curious disciple.

"With My heavenly Father," was the answer.

For Nathanael, new vistas of being and of time suddenly brushed into his consciousness. But an obvious question arises: How could Jesus sustain such a claim? To claim to have no beginning is one thing; to make it reasonable is another. If heaven is the point of reference for all of reality, then two major ramifications were entailed for the disciples, and therefore, also are for us. The first is that of position with reference to Him and the second, that of position with reference to us. The second logically follows from the first.

What do I mean by position? I mean the very vantage point from which I may now view life because of Him.

Have you ever experienced the confusion of a seemingly senseless config-uration on a poster that appears to be random shapes or dots? As you con-tinue to stare at it and tilt your head one way or the other, a word or a picture suddenly leaps out from that cluttered pattern. We call it a cryptogram.

Something fascinating happens once you have seen that the dots or shad-ing were just masking the real message. You start tilting your head in various positions in an attempt to lose the ordered pattern and to regain the initial disorder. The latter exercise comes into play only because you start wonder-ing how it was possible in the first place to miss the word. When the eye has captured the image, it interprets the message for what it is. When the eye loses the message, disarray dominates.

May I suggest that the challenge of Jesus' earthly ministry was to enable us to see the message so that the picture could be understood. Staring at life's cryptogram, we either see His name unmistakably resplendent or we see the confusion of religions with no single message, just garbled beliefs that plague our existence, each justified by the voice of culture. That may be the tragedy of the beguiling sentiment we call tolerance, which has become a euphemism for contradiction. The result is treacherous.

Jesus Christ came to challenge every culture on the face of the earth so that we might gain a perspective from higher ground. But how does one reach that higher ground? We can see the hint of our predicament even from our lower vantage point. In spite of the limitations of our earthbound perspective, we still recognize wickedness. We still talk of witnessing evil. Maybe, there is a reason. C. S. Lewis helps us here:

> Heaven understands hell and hell does not understand heaven. . . . To project ourselves into a wicked character, we have only to stop doing something and something we are already tired of doing; to project ourselves into a good one we have to do what we cannot and become what we are not.[1]

"To do what we cannot and to become what we are not." Those limitations separate purity from evil. To change this, heaven's eyes must be planted in us. That is what Jesus offers the one who comes to Him—to be what in ourselves we cannot be and to do what by ourselves we cannot do.

As a young lad, I remember reading a story about Sir Isaac Newton that left a profound impression on me. He had worked for hours on his scientific inquiries into the very core of the physical universe, exhaustedly laboring by candlelight. By his side over the weeks sat his beloved dog.

On one occasion when Newton left the room for a moment, the dog jumped up to follow him and inadvertently bumped into the side of the desk, knocking over the candle and setting the papers ablaze. All that seminal work was reduced in moments to a pile of ashes.

When Newton returned to his study to see what remained of his work, his heart was broken beyond repair. Rescuing what little was left of the room, he sat down and wept with his face in his hands. Gently stroking the dog, he said, "You will never, never know what you have done."

Even if it were possible for the dog to grasp that something tragic had happened, it was impossible for the creature to know the *kind* of tragedy, not just the degree of what had been done.

By analogy, that kind of essential distance is what makes our situation so manifestly impossible. Living in an evil world makes it much easier for me to understand my own wickedness than to think in the crystal-clear terms of perfect purity. In his biography of Mother Teresa, Christopher Hitchens set out as his goal to find something that would mar her character. He said of Mother Teresa, "She is the great white whale for the atheist in me."[2] So he had to play Ahab and bleed her.

How revealing that is of human nature. We resent the indictment purity brings. Is it any wonder that we cannot understand God? This gap is not only one of morality; it is one of capacity. It is easier for me to think in terms of time than for me to think in terms of eternity. How can I ever explain the dwelling of a perfect Being in eternity when my being is so locked into imperfection and time? How can I understand the supernatural when I am so bound by the natural?

There is a German term that separates existence from life: *dasein ohne leben*—"existence without life." Jesus came to remind us that we who are bound to the temporal subsist without life's blueprint. Though we continue to exist, we miss life for what it was meant to be. He wants us to see what it means to live through the lens of the eternal. That takes place when He makes our lives His home. There, He has promised to bless us.

Jesus once said to someone who questioned Him, "I have spoken to you of earthly things and you do not believe; how then will you believe if I speak of heavenly things?" (John 3:12).

Is this distinctive of Christ's heavenly dwelling a unique factor in world religions? Indeed it is. Perhaps this unequaled credential of Jesus may be in the minds of Muslim scholars when they attempt to attribute to Mohammed a momentary excursion into heaven. Islam claims that at one point in his life, on one particular night, Mohammed was transported to heaven on a single journey, to be given a glimpse of what heaven is like.[3] Regardless of all the confusing arguments over this claim, it does establish that even if the text is taken at face value, what warranted the heavenward journey for a night was that heaven was foreign to Mohammed. And that is the point of difference.

With such a unique difference, the skeptic may ask a legitimate question. Is there any evidence that can be adduced to support Jesus' claim of origin?

CONCEPTION WITHOUT CONSUMMATION

If Jesus had no beginning, then His very birth must explain how He could be "born" and yet not have a beginning. The virgin birth of Jesus most certainly addresses that.

When one is searching for evidence to confirm a startling claim, it is necessary to look for some other source that gives credence to it, even though it would not be in its own best interests to do so. The virgin birth is certainly in that realm, both for those who experienced it and for those inimical to the gospel. For Mary herself to claim such an outlandish conception would have been to not only risk her own life, but also to have put Jesus' life at risk.

Though I have quoted this numerous times before, I would like to repeat it here. The popular talk-show host Larry King was once asked whom he would choose, if he had the choice to interview one person across history. Larry King replied that he would like to interview Jesus Christ and that he would ask Him just one question: "Are You indeed virgin born?" "The answer to that question," said King, "would explain history for me."[4]

Larry King is right. The virgin birth at the very least points to a world unbound by sheer naturalism. The claim is lofty, but think it through even in its original and early context. Jesus' virgin birth was claimed while giving it the clear possibility of being verified along many lines.

Of any influential life that you have witnessed or studied, ask yourself how this person would justify a virgin birth and an eternal existence, if such an assertion were being made. This would be a particularly significant question if it had been predicted before the person was born. How do you perfectly fit together prophecy—in fact, hundreds of prophecies—and its fulfillment? For Jesus' antagonists, it would have been easy to measure, generation by generation, whether this claim to be the Messiah could possibly have withstood the scholars' scrutiny and the Scriptures' test. That is why the genealogies were far more important for the early disciples than the furniture in the house.

Apart from Mary and Joseph, consider the testimonies of Zacharias the priest and his wife, Elizabeth (the parents of John the Baptizer), for whom it would have been natural not to want their son to play "second fiddle" to a cousin, especially a younger cousin. In a culture rife with power and position, where the home bespoke volumes, shame would not be the path of choice for anyone. Had the virgin birth not been true, to assert its truth was the path of cultural ostracism, if not suicide, for all of them. For Elizabeth to lose her son, John, to the sword of Herod and for Mary to be told by the angel that a sword would pierce through her heart would not have been desired by any mother. Mary, Joseph, Zacharias, Elizabeth, John, and then the disciples risked everything for this truth.

But even beyond the Hebrew disposition and the family's claim, possibly the most astounding affirmation of the virgin birth comes from one religion that for centuries has attempted to stand against the Christian gospel, Islam. Even the Koran, written six hundred years after Jesus, affirmed His virgin birth (see Surah 19.19–21). This would serve Islam no self-glorifying purpose.

Here, then, is the man from Nazareth, who claimed that His origin was from heaven and that His Father is none other than God Himself—a Son not born out of physical consummation nor out of a need for communion, but the consummate expression of God in the flesh, in eternal communion with the Father.

His birth was not by natural means. This cannot be said of Mohammed, Krishna, or Buddha. Islam, while defending the virgin birth, denies that Jesus was the Son of God. It has, therefore, never been able to break free from a contradiction of its own making on the matter of Jesus' sonship. Its assertion that it is blasphemous to suggest that God could have a Son is based on their notion that sexual union is necessary for a child to be born, and of course, that would demean God. So there is a half-truth here, with an ironic twist for a religion whose founding prophet had numerous sexual unions, all, they claim, instigated by God. But that aside, if they have already granted the virgin birth, then they have acknowledged that God, in His infinite power, can initiate life without sexual union. In the beginning, communion and the power to give life existed in God Himself. In His infinite being, relationship was intrinsic, without the fleshly prerequisite of physical consummation. God, who is Spirit, is, in fact, Being-in-relationship. In Christ, the Word *became* flesh. He alone, who dwelt in eternity, could consecrate the flesh while differentiating between the inherent power of creation and the bestowed power of procreation, even as He transcended the means by which we are bound.

A Life without Blemish

But there was a second way in which Jesus proved His absolute and eternal existence. His life has always been regarded as the purest that has ever been lived. On numerous occasions, His antagonists were challenged to bring some contrary proof against Him. They were never able to besmirch His pristine life. He challenged His adversaries to lay any charge of sin at His feet. As we progress in this book, we will see how hard they tried.

By contrast, no other individual has ever elicited such accolades. By their own admission, this includes Mohammed, Buddha, and Krishna. Their lives and their struggles are recorded within their own scriptures. Throughout the Muslim world today the belief is held that all of the prophets were sinless. One marvels at this doctrine, as it was never a view of the prophets presented in the Old Testament nor is it evident in their own scriptures. The shortcomings of two of the most renowned and respected prophets in Islam, Abraham and Moses, are plainly stated in the Koran. For example in Surah 28,16 Moses asked for forgiveness after slaying the Egyptian. In Surah 26,82 Abraham asked for forgiveness on the Day of Judgment. The word used here, which Muslims translate as "fault" rather than "sin," is the same word that in other contexts they translate as "sin."

In Surahs 47 and 48, Mohammed himself was told to ask for forgiveness for sin, once again translated as "faults" rather than "sin." Again, the word that is used in Surah 47,19 is the same word that is translated as "sin" in

Surah 12,29, where it is applied to Potiphar's wife in her attempted seduction of Joseph. Numerous linguists see this attempt to bypass what is really being said as nothing short of the development of a tradition so that Mohammed's life did not suffer in contrast to Jesus'.

There is great diversity in the attempts to explain this away. But what is a "fault" that needs forgiving? Is it something that ought to be a certain way but is not? Is it a thought that was entertained in error?

There is much more that can be said by way of contrast between the lives of Mohammed and Jesus. Mohammed's marriages to eleven wives have been a fascinating subject for Muslim scholars to explain. Whatever else a marriage does or does not prove, it clearly establishes the gradual need to die to one's self so that the two can become one. It is a process of failing and picking up, never one of perfection. But even if one were to grant all of the strained explanations for Mohammed's practices, included in which is the embarrassing Koranic description of heaven as "wine and women" (Surah 78.32ff, which Muslims dismiss as metaphorical), there is never even a hint in the life of Jesus that He was ever driven by sensuality or needed to seek forgiveness for anything. Jesus alone emerges as the spotless One, untainted by any error of omission or commission.

It should also be noted that this contrast is not only evident in the way Jesus and Mohammed lived, but also in the way they understood their call. So different is this sense of origin and call that, by Islam's own accounts, when Mohammed first claimed to have received revelations, he was confused and not sure what it meant. It was others who told him that this could be the voice of God speaking to him. Jesus, on the other hand, knew exactly who He was and from whence He came.

Hinduism is not exempt from this scrutiny. The playfulness of Krishna and his exploits with the milkmaids in the Bhagavad-Gita is frankly an embarrassment to many Hindu scholars.

How does Buddha measure up against the standard of personal purity that Jesus set? The very fact that he endured rebirths implies a series of imperfect lives. When he left his home in the palace, turning his back on his wife and son, it was in search of an answer. He did not start with the answer. His

"Enlightenment" was an attainment. Even taken at face value, it was a *path* to purity, not purity per se.

Jesus did not begin His mission by leaving more comfortable surroundings in order to gain enlightenment so that He would find the answer to life's mysteries. That was the origin of Buddhism.

He did not come to give a certain group of people ethnic worth so that they, too, could have an identity as others around them did; Islam had its beginnings for such reasons.[5]

He did not give any people a reason to boast of particular privilege because of the age of their culture or the perceived strength of their society's cohesion; virtually all pantheistic cultures pride themselves on how long they have been in existence.

He did not come to affirm a people who boasted in the strength of their military power, as the citizens of Rome did in claiming their city to be the eternal city.

He did not come to compliment the Greeks for their intellectual prowess.

In fact, He did not even come to exalt a culture because it was the recipient of God's moral law, a boast the Hebrews delighted in.

His strong and unequivocal claim was that heaven was His dwelling and earth was His footstool. There never was a time when He was not. There never will be a time when He will not be. His was a positing of truth from an eternal perspective that uniquely positioned Him.

Changing Our Address

I said earlier that not only was our position of vision affected, but our very place in life was redefined. If the privilege of Jesus' position gives us His unique vantage point, sustained by His supernatural birth, then one very necessary application follows if we are to apply His truth to our homes.

The implication was clearly a surprise to Nathanael, for whom nothing good could come out of Nazareth. Nazareth was hardly on the map. It took scholars years even to pinpoint Nazareth. Of all the places on earth, why would the Lord of heaven and earth choose Nazareth? Is it possible that since heaven was His abode and earth was His footstool, He chose the foot of the footstool so that those of us who pride ourselves on our birth may take note that our heavenly Father has better credentials for us than our earthly roots?

Our world has strayed so far from God's will for us that we have made ourselves wretched by measuring ourselves in terms of race or power or progress or learning. The flames of prejudice of every kind have burned through twenty centuries. The politicization and absolutizing of culture may well be the cause of our next worldwide conflagration. All of the privileges of birth and possession become destructive when they are unhinged from our Creator's moorings.

The words of Jesus are a stirring reminder to all of us that the pride of birth carried to extreme can be a vortex that sucks us into destructive ways of thinking and living. The rising voice of nationalism has unleashed horrors too numerous to mention. In years of travel, I have been to many places in the world where people think they are superior because of their culture, places like China, the Middle East, Europe, and America. One way or the other, we all think we are the center of the universe because of our place in life. We had absolutely nothing to do with our birth. Jesus did, and He chose a most unlikely city to call home. He was not ensnared by the flimsy and fickle attachments of nationalism.

But if culture or birth must never give way to prejudice, neither must wealth become a means of measuring essential worth. I find the silence of Scripture on Jesus' economic conditions at home to be very instructive. In a culture where location and city meant so much, the only hint we are given as it applies to Jesus is that He came from unexpected economic ranks. I believe it is a solemn reminder not to make our goal in life one of sheer material pursuit. The allurement is great, and the disappointments are proportionate.

I recall reading, in one of New York's leading newspapers, an interview with the wife of a New York Yankees ballplayer who had just signed an $89 million contract. He had held out for a long while before signing, hoping that the management would match the $91 million offer of another team. The Yankees did not budge. His wife later said, "When I saw him walk in the house, I immediately knew that he had not succeeded in persuading them to move up from eighty-nine to ninety-one million. He felt so rejected. It was one of the saddest days of our lives."

Such, alas, are the vagaries of the human mind.

Most of us will never have our hearts broken because we were offered a paltry eighty-nine million instead of the ninety-one million we wanted. But many of us do lose our way within our own material contexts. It is not the size of the check that messes us up; it is our priorities. I do not believe for a moment that the Scriptures are against wealth. But the warning to those who make wealth their pursuit is a stern reality. Wealth must be processed through a philosophy of life that is greater than wealth itself. If not, it shapes the mind for bitter disappointments. Over the years, God has given me the privilege of being with some who are naturally gifted in multiplying what has been entrusted to them. Many have admitted to me that learning to walk with wealth is a very difficult discipline.

Nikos Kazantzakis was thoroughly wrong about Jesus in his book *The Last Temptation of Christ.* He presented a scene in which Satan passed before Jesus' imagination what He could have had if He had resisted the cross—a home in Bethany, the enthrallment of a wife in Mary or Martha, or both! Kazantzakis was wrong. Dead wrong. He never paused to reflect that a home in Bethany would not exactly be an allurement to One whose dwelling was in heaven.

I bring this chapter and its lessons to a close with a personal memory. Some years ago, we were spending Christmas in the home of my wife's parents. It was not a happy day in the household. Much had gone wrong during the preceding weeks, and a weight of sadness hung over the home. Yet, in the midst of all that, my mother-in-law kept her routine habit of asking people who would likely have no place to go at Christmas to share Christmas dinner with us.

That year she invited a man who was, by everyone's estimation, somewhat of an odd person, quite eccentric in his demeanor. Not much was known about him at the church except that he came regularly, sat alone, and left without much conversation. He obviously lived alone and was quite a sorry-looking, solitary figure. He was our Christmas guest.

Because of other happenings in the house, not the least of which was that one daughter was taken to the hospital for the birth of her first child, everything was confusion. All of our emotions were on edge. It fell upon me, in turn, to entertain this gentleman. I must confess that I did not appreciate it. Owing to a heavy life of travel year-round, I have jealously guarded my Christmases to be with my family. This was not going to be such a privilege, and I was not happy. As I sat in the living room, entertaining him while others were busy, I thought to myself, *This is going to go down as one of the most miserable Christmases of my life.*

But somehow we got through the evening. He evidently loved the meal, the fire crackling in the background, the snow outside, the Christmas carols playing, and a rather weighty theological discussion in which he and I were engaged—at his instigation, I might add. He was a very well-read man and, as I found out, loved to grapple with heavy theological themes. I do, too, but frankly, not during an evening that has been set aside to enjoy life's quiet moments, not someone's polemical mind.

At the end of the night when he bade us all good-bye, he reached out and took the hand of each of us, one by one, and said, "Thank you for the best Christmas of my life. I will never forget it." He walked out into the dark, snowy night, back into his solitary existence.

My heart sank in self-indictment at those tender words of his. I had to draw on every nerve in my being to keep from breaking down with tears. Just a few short years later, relatively young, and therefore to our surprise, he passed away. I have relived that Christmas many times in my memory.

The Lord taught me a lesson. The primary purpose of a home is to reflect and to distribute the love of Christ. Anything that usurps that is idolatrous. Having been lifted beyond the prejudice of culture, Jesus repositioned for the disciples the place of wealth. So staggering was the impact that many of them in the years to come would leave their own homes to go to distant parts of the world in order to proclaim the heaven-sent message that redefined their earthly homes. Eleven of them paid for that message with their lives.

The first time I walked through the noisy streets of Bethlehem and endured its smells, I gained a whole new sense of the difference between our Christmas carols, glamorizing the sweetness of the "little town of Bethlehem," and the harsh reality of God becoming flesh and dwelling among us. Ah! But is it not part of the wonder of God's disclosure of reality that He points to what we live with to show us what true living is meant to be?

For the disciples, Jesus' answer to their simple question—"Where do You live?"—was to lift them beyond race and culture, beyond wealth and power, beyond time and distance to make them true citizens of the world, informed by the world to come. He brought them into a dramatically different way of living and thinking from the one to which they were accustomed. He showed them the inclusiveness of His love for the whole world. But implicit in that was the exclusivity of His truth, for which they were willing to give their lives. We have reversed Jesus' order. We have made truth relative and culture supreme and have been left with a world in which wickedness reigns.

Jesus brought truth to light and a different world to His message. In Him my heart finds its true home.

G. K. Chesterton has captured the wonder in how Jesus' earthly address changes ours, as only he can do.

> A child in a foul stable,
> Where the beasts feed and foam;
> Only where He was homeless
> Are you and I at home:
> We have hands that fashion and heads that know,
> But our hearts we lost—how long ago!
> In a place no chart nor ship can show
> Under the sky's dome.
> To an open house in the evening
> Home shall men come,
> To an older place than Eden
> And a taller town than Rome.
> To the end of the way of the wandering star,
> To the things that cannot be and that are,
> To the place where God was homeless
> And all men are at home.[6]

Where does Jesus live? Come to Christ and see what it means to live.

Chapter Three

THE ANATOMY OF FAITH AND THE QUEST FOR REASON

THE NOTED ATHEISTIC PHILOSOPHER BERTRAND RUSSELL WAS ONCE asked, "If you meet God after you die, what will you say to Him to justify your unbelief?"

"I will tell Him that He did not give me enough evidence," Russell snapped.

Bertrand Russell may have been an unusually hostile voice against all religious belief, and Christianity in particular, but his thirst for evidence or his demand for proof is not unique.

For my part, I confess that I wonder more about those who seek no such support for the things they believe than about those who do. There are hundreds, if not thousands, whose paths I have crossed in my journeys who have not only "theoretically believed" in some divine entity, but have also made their commitment with heartfelt devotion. "Gods" and "goddesses" with ghastly features and attributes are venerated by millions bringing their offerings and prostrating themselves in worship. I am confounded by such unquestioning commitment, practiced because of a feeling that is engendered or is the bequest of their culture.

On the other hand, I also grant that finding a hard-nosed rational justification for belief can be a tedious and sometimes hazardous pursuit. But if truth is the motive for the search, when reasonably pursued, it has its rewards. There is an old adage that says, "It is better to debate a question before settling it than to settle a question before debating it." My own intellectual battles were rather necessary in a land filled with as many "gods" as people.

Unfortunately, for reasons justifiable and unjustifiable, individuals hostile to belief in God often malign faith in Him as the lure of emotion clinging to an idea with the mind disengaged. They do not believe that faith can sustain the weight of both the emotions and the mind.

I realize we are all built with different capacities for thinking on such matters. However, that will not serve as reason enough to support one view over another. We cannot evade the questions that opponents have posed to those who "live by faith." They are justified in wanting to know what distinguishes faith from foolishness or irrationality, when no coherent logic is ever offered for one's "faith."

My mother, in great frustration, on one occasion asked me, "From where do you come up with all these questions? Must there be an explanation for everything?" I envied her simplicity. But our idiosyncrasies aside, I have to raise the counterpoint in a world plagued with contradicting ways of defining ultimate reality. To commit one's life, habits, thoughts, goals, priorities—everything—to a certain world-view with no questions asked is, from the antagonist's point of view, to build one's life upon a very questionable foundation.

In this encounter with Jesus, we will deal with a hard question that was asked of Him, and we will see as a result both the anatomy of faith and the quest for reason. Indeed, Jesus warned the seekers of signs in very serious terms. But He also justified His claims in extraordinary ways. There is a balance, and we must find it.

Some years ago, while in the Philippines speaking at some meetings, I was staying at a small, family-run hotel. The woman who managed the place had a graduate degree in philosophy and struck up quite a conversation with me on the rationality or irrationality of belief in God. During the conversation, she asked me if I had met a particular family staying in that hotel, who had come from Australia to have their son cured of cancer by a "faith healer."

Eventually, one evening I found myself in the room of this couple, with their young son. I cannot at this point recall his exact age, but I believe he was somewhere between ten and twelve years old. He lay in his narrow bed, emaciated, motionless, and pitiful, almost lifeless. His face, ashen gray, was drawn with the look of death. His parents and I talked in low tones in that small room. By his side was a night table, on which was a jar with some murky liquid and a frightful-looking purple fleshy mass that sprouted hairy roots.

The boy's mother pointed to it and asked me, "Do you see what is in that jar?"

I nodded.

"That is the cancer that the faith healer removed without surgery. It is like magic. We are sure that our son is now healed."

I just stared at them with heaviness of heart, thinking of their terrible pain. At the same time it was extremely difficult to be face to face with such credulity, looking into the eyes of those who were willing to put the life of their child into the hands of such claimants to the miraculous, many of whom are known charlatans. There, against all outward signs, two educated and well-to-do people boasted a cure from one who muttered an incantation and supposedly, without making any incision, extracted this fist-sized thing that was "causing the cancer" in their son. How does one explain this extreme form of "faith"? The human capacity to believe the bizarre, especially in the face of dire need, is limitless.

I have no doubt that in the Scriptures God often intervened in the healing of the body many times and that He continues to do so today. But this episode was a far cry from that, for here the mercenary and cultic elements were too obvious to miss.

Before I left, I explained to them that my work took me into many parts of the world and that it would really help me to know if the power of that healer were real or devious. "I would greatly appreciate you doing me the favor of writing to me within a month or two and telling me if your son has been truly healed," I said. They took my address and promised they would write. That was more than a decade ago. I have never heard anything from them.

If isolated instances demand that we not risk our lives on the preposterous claims of some self-styled demagogue, how much more important it is that we not risk the very destiny of humanity on someone who insists that He is the only true answer to life's purpose and destiny—unless that claim can be thoroughly tested and justified. Interestingly enough, to those like Bertrand Russell who contend that there is a paucity of evidence, the Bible makes a staggering counterpoint. The Scriptures categorically state that the problem with such people is not the absence of evidence; it is, rather, the *suppression* of it. The message of Jesus Christ shifts the charge of insufficiency from the volume of evidence to the intent of one's will.

Was Jesus implying that belief is nothing more than a blind commitment of the will? I think not. But He did say, in effect, that if you test His claims by the same measure that you legitimately substantiate other facts, you will find Him and His teaching thoroughly trustworthy. The evidence is already there. The denial of Christ has less to do with facts and more to do with the bent of what a person is prejudiced to conclude. After years of wrestling with such issues in academia, I have seen this proven time and again.

Notice, for example, the words of Thomas Nagel, professor of philosophy at New York University. This is how he explains his deep-seated antipathy toward religion:

> In speaking of the fear of religion, I don't mean to refer to the entirely reasonable hostility toward certain established religions . . . in virtue of their objectionable moral doctrines, social policies, and political influence. Nor am I referring to the association of many religious beliefs with superstition and the acceptance of evident empirical falsehoods. I am talking about something much deeper—namely the fear of religion itself. . . . I want atheism to be true and am made uneasy by the fact that some of the most intelligent and well-informed people I know are religious believers. It isn't just that I don't believe in God and naturally, hope there is no God! I don't want there to be a God; I don't want the universe to be like that.[1]

That is unabashed, committed unbelief. "I don't want there to be a God." While Bertrand Russell's skepticism may be represented as the honest search of reason, we had better be sure that it is not actually the wanton unbelief of Thomas Nagel that lurks beneath that intellectual quest. That kind of skepticism is the distortion of reason, masquerading as candor. To such a disposition, nothing would serve as sufficient evidence. We will find that as we study this theme of reason and faith and the place of the sign, God has much more to say about it than we realize.

NOTHING NEW IN THE DEMAND

Long before our modern skeptics demanded evidence, the most religiously minded of their day came to Jesus and asked, "What miraculous sign can you show us to prove your authority to do all this?" (John 2:18).

They were not the Russells and Nagels of their day, lambasting the supernatural. In fact, they were a vital part of the life of the temple, which was at once the religious and mercenary ocean into which all of their efforts flowed. Tables were set up within its grounds from which to sell and profit from the people's desire to be right with God. From sacrificial lambs to trinkets, the exploiters and the exploited kept it a busy place, humming and buzzing with the sounds of eternal and temporal fears. The physically deprived and disabled would come as close as they were permitted to, in search of healing and restoration. Keepers of the moral law, the ceremonial law, and laws of their own invention found the temple to be their salvation.

Of all the enterprises in which the human heart engages, none lends itself more to abuse and manipulation than the activities of religion. For here, sacrifice and greed can meet in the most trusting and exploiting context. The much-respected scholar and one-time missionary Stephen Neill once said, "I am inclined to think that ambition in any ordinary sense of the term is nearly always sinful in ordinary men. I am certain that in the Christian it is always sinful, and that it is most inexcusable of all in the ordained minister."[2]

I believe that Neill was right. From Voltaire to Einstein, thinkers have heaped grave suspicion on institutional religion because of its checkered past. It is a tragedy that the history of religion, Christianity included, is filled with so much abuse that skeptics are very often justified in their "rational rejection" of the message. Jesus bore the brunt of the anger of the ecclesiastical authorities when He reminded them that their duplicity was the cause of unbelief in the masses.

It was in such a confrontation between Jesus and the guardians of the temple that the demand for a sign came. On a given day and at an appointed time, Jesus walked into the temple and flipped over the tables of the peddlers of religious paraphernalia and drove them out of there. "Get these out of here! How dare you turn my Father's house into a market!" (John 2:16). They had transformed a place of worship into a hangout for crooks.

In a certain part of the world that I have visited often, right outside the hotel is a little shrine. I have watched every morning, as thousands walked by. Most would pause, bow, fold their hands, or make some kind of a reverential sign to honor the deity and then move on. Many of those who ceremoniously carried out that ritual would then walk a few paces and "lie in wait" to see which tourists they could hoodwink that morning. From unfurling nude pictures or offering the services of a prostitute, to selling fake Rolex watches for twenty dollars, their day was spent in the illegal and the immoral. They were zealous and aggressive in leading the gullible astray.

As I have pondered this, I have tried to put together their habits of worship and their scandalous business. I have come to the conclusion that *hypocrite* is a very innocuous word to describe such a life. Their activities, both sacred and perverse, were not hidden—they were all done in the open. I believe that what has actually happened is a cutting of the nerve of spirituality at the neck, so that it never filters down to the heart, hands, and feet. Life is lived out in self-contained compartments with nothing to connect them. Their bowing recognizes the sacred. Their exploiting grants the material. In living, they desecrate others without a twinge of conscience. Yet if anyone were to hint at desecrating that shrine, his life would be in peril. Such is the amputation of religion that pays homage to God but would be the most surprised if God were ever to show up.

To such a band of thugs, Jesus came. It was an unprecedented confrontation. To borrow current-day jargon—"Politically incorrect" would be a lamblike description for a lionlike act. To run afoul of the powerbrokers and to refer to the temple as His Father's house? Both the deed and the words were shocking to the observers. This event was to burn itself into the memories of the onlookers and sealed His adversaries in their determination to do away with Him. As the disciples watched the entire episode, they were terribly nervous. But the account tells us that a voice from the past pierced their consciences. They suddenly remembered a passage of Scripture penned by King David one thousand years earlier: "I am a stranger to my brothers, an alien to my own mother's sons; for zeal for your house consumes me, and the insults of those who insult you fall on me" (Ps. 69:8–9). Jesus, they took note, embodied that prediction.

His antagonists could not contain their rage and demanded that Jesus give them a sign to justify His daring action. He only annoyed them further by countering that their question was anything but a quest for truth. But He did not end there. In His answer, He offered proof that no other claimant to Messianic or divine office has ever fulfilled. For so great a challenge, it was going to take an unparalleled demonstration of power.

A New Response

"Destroy this temple, and I will raise it again in three days" (John 2:19).

"What?" they countered. "It has taken forty-six years to build this temple, and you are going to raise it in three days?" (v. 20).

The Gospel writer adds, "The temple he had spoken of was his body. After he was raised from the dead, his disciples recalled what he had said. Then they believed the Scripture and the words that Jesus had spoken" (vv. 21–22).

There are so many different ways in which He could have shown His authority. He chose one particular point of reference—the temple. But He incorporated into that metaphor a meaning that would address both the skeptic and the religious person alike. For in the human body lie opposite possibilities: our propensities for the sensate and the willingness even to disfigure the body for the sake of the spiritual. Jesus could not have chosen a better illustration to justify His authority than His reference to the body in connection with the temple.

There are at least three distinct facets to His answer.

To see the first facet, we need to look at the *pretext* that the skeptic brought to the verbal exchange. "What sign do You offer for Your authority?" In this challenge, we will see the conflict of faith and reason.

The second is the *text* with which Jesus responded: "Destroy this temple and in three days I will raise it up." In time, this was going to be the single greatest proof of His claim. Centuries of determination to try to prove Him spurious have only strengthened His proof.

The last facet of Jesus' answer is the *context* within which He wanted the implication of His message understood. He offered the ultimate miracle by taking that which posed the greatest threat to spiritual inclination and translating it into the center of spirituality. In time, they would recognize that His answer was unique and was sustained in history.

THE SEDUCTION AND DEDUCTION OF A SIGN

Let us first grapple with the *pretext* of the skeptic.

One may be surprised to hear that history does not have a long list of serious claimants to divine status. What has resulted, however, is the gradual manufacturing of divinity by human choice. That list is ponderous.

On one occasion I stood by the side of a road, watching the golden statue of a "god" being transported from one temple to another. Thousands clamored to give an offering and to receive a blessing. The priests accompanying the god had incense and ash in their hands and generously distributed the goodwill of the deity upon any fruit or piece of clothing placed before them. The sight was extraordinary. Rich, poor, young, and old stretched their hands up as this chariot went by at a snail's pace. I asked a woman who had just received her "blessing" if this god actually existed or if he was just an expression of some inner hunger. She looked very hesitant and then said, "If you think in your heart that he exists, then he does."

"What if you believe he does not exist?" I asked.

"Then he doesn't exist," she softly said. That possibly summarizes the major personages to whom divinity is ascribed today. Some will attempt to prove their beliefs; others just quietly carry them in their hearts, creating deities whom they then try to appease.

Common sense dictates that in asserting a conviction of belief, we do more than offer a heart's desire or present some isolated strands of the claimant's credentials with which to leap to grandiose conclusions. A true defense of any claim must also deal with the evidences that challenge or contradict it. In other words, truth is not only a matter of offense, in that it makes certain assertions. It is also a matter of defense, in that it must be able to make a cogent and sensible response to the counterpoints that are raised.

And here something very important surfaces. Sometimes the choice is not between that which is manifestly contradictory and that which is consistently coherent. To contrast the former cult leader Jim Jones with Jesus Christ is not difficult. The challenge emerges when a claimant to deity may have some unique features that attract, while covering up a multitude of contradictory teachings or a contradicting lifestyle.

Unsuspecting people make a fatal mistake when they give their allegiance to a system of thought by focusing on its benefits while they ignore its systemic contradictions. The entire life of anyone making prophetic or divine claims must be observed in concert with the teaching offered. Numerous historical and philosophical matters come into play when one seriously evaluates such claims.

This is precisely what makes Jesus so unique. The whole range of both His life and His teaching can be subjected to the test of truth. Each aspect of His teaching is a link in the greater whole. Each facet is like the face of a diamond, catching the light as it is gently turned.

We assume, at this time in the history of thought, that the ancients were more gullible than we and that we have come of age when, in truth, some of the credulity we have displayed would have rightly made them squirm. If anyone denies that reality, just ask those in the marketing industry whether it is form or substance that sells. Several times in the Gospels someone in the audience challenged Jesus to give a sign in order to prove His claims. They were not a naive bunch. It is telling that in virtually every instance, the challenge came on the heels of a miraculous act that Jesus had just performed. They were not even satisfied merely to see the miraculous. They wanted something more.

For example, in John 6:30, the demand for a sign follows His feeding of five thousand people from a handful of loaves and fishes. Immediately after the miracle the skeptics in the group reminded Jesus that Moses had fed the masses with manna. "What miraculous sign then will *you* give that we may see it and believe you?" (emphasis added). In Matthew's Gospel, the demand for a sign came after the healing of a blind and mute man (12:22–45).

These give us clues to what Jesus was up against and why He responded the way He did. When the Pharisees and the teachers of the law demanded a sign of Him in Matthew 12, He replied with some rather pointed words:

> A wicked and adulterous generation asks for a miraculous sign! But none will be given it except the sign of the prophet Jonah. . . . The men of Nineveh will stand up at the judgment with this generation and condemn it; for they repented at the preaching of Jonah, and now one greater than Jonah is here. The Queen of the South will rise at the judgment with this generation and condemn it; for she came from the ends of the earth to listen to Solomon's wisdom, and now one greater than Solomon is here. (vv. 39, 41–42)

Jesus is charging that the very motivation that impelled them to demand a sign revealed not only that they were not genuinely seeking the truth; their resistance to truth, though they were religious, made the hardened pagan look better than they. In other words, it was not the absence of a sign that troubled them. It was the *message* behind the signs that provoked their discomfort. If Jesus could sustain who He was, the ramifications for them were cataclysmic. Everything they pursued and owned, every vestige of inordinate power they enjoyed, was dependent on their being the determiners of other people's destinies. Sometimes religion can be the greatest roadblock to true spirituality.

The bitter tip of Jesus' verbal arrow struck a raw nerve in them when He said that even a murderous people like the Ninevites were more honest than they were. Why? Because Jonah's preaching to the Ninevites resulted in a national repentance on such a scale that it made history. And Solomon's wisdom was so widely recognized that it brought people from distant lands just to listen to him.

In brief, Jesus is saying that a message in itself won the hearts of the pagans, but those who claimed spiritual fervor were fleeing from the implications of what they already knew to be true. He demonstrated more authenticating signs and persuasions than Jonah, more beauty and wisdom in thought than Solomon. Jonah was not the author of the miraculous. Jesus was. Solomon was not the source of His wisdom. Jesus was. Yet that difference counted as nothing to them.

From then on, all the way to His death on the cross at their hands, Jesus proved that it was not evidence they were looking for, but control of their enterprises, even at the cost of truth.

I would venture to suggest that the skepticism of some in our time may well come from the same motivation. A major difference for the average person of our day from the context of Jesus' day is that He was trying to establish Himself as Messiah to an audience that at least believed in the existence of God. In our day, we must first establish the existence of God. Only then can we present the evidence that Jesus is God incarnate.

To the religiously minded, the challenge is more complex. How do we establish that Jesus is the only way to God? Where do we find the common ground on which to begin?

FAITH AND REASON

Faith has not always been as suspect a category as it has now come to be. Both the Hebrews and the Greeks had an understanding of faith. True, there were some differences, but faith still had legitimacy. Today, if faith is admitted at all, it is seen as the faith to have faith. It is packaged as a private matter and banned from intellectual credence.

"Everyone has to have some faith," we quip.

"If it were not for my faith, I would never have hung in there," we may hear someone else say.

Faith in what, one might ask? In such a faith, the focus is often on anything but truth and on everything that signals pragmatism—"It worked for me, whether it's true or not." Such glib pronouncements have made us vulnerable to the faith marketers of our time. It is time to do some "temple cleansing" of the mind and face this reality head-on.

First, let us clearly understand what faith is not before establishing what it is. The faith that the Bible speaks of is not antithetical to reason. It is not just a will to believe, everything to the contrary notwithstanding. It is not a predisposition to force every piece of information to fit into the mold of one's desires. Faith in the biblical sense is substantive, based on the knowledge that the One in whom that faith is placed has proven that He is worthy of that trust. In its essence, *faith is a confidence in the person of Jesus Christ and in His power, so that even when His power does not serve my end, my confidence in Him remains because of who He is.* Faith for the Christian is the response of trust based on who Jesus Christ claimed to be, and it results in a life that brings both mind and heart in a commitment of love to Him. Is this an irrational or unreasonable response based on all that Christ demonstrated Himself to be?

Each individual who comes into this kind of faith in the one true God does so through a different struggle. In the Old Testament, Moses was the classic example of how faith was built into someone for whom the implications of trust were not easy. Repeatedly and protractedly, God pursued Moses until Moses understood that the God he served expected his trust and that He would prove Himself, both before and after the trust had been followed through. God gave him just enough, along his journey, to demonstrate who He was but saved the climactic proof for the end of Moses' journey of faith.

On the other hand, Abraham is shown to us as one who so hungered after God that he was willing, with minimal outward proof, to leave his home and to build for posterity a community of faith in the living God. But even in his case, every step in his faith-building process was met with the affirmation of God. God deals with both kinds of us, those of us who long for more evidence and those of us for whom a little evidence will do. But He works always in concert with a revelation of His character.

But notice that there are twin angles here. The first is that of trust. Jesus claimed to be the consummate expression of God. The true believer trusts Him to be speaking the truth. Everything He said and did sustains that claim, and contrarily, nothing He said or did challenges that claim. It has been said that human nature abhors a vacuum, and that must be true of our faith too. None of us live comfortably with a vacuous faith. There ought to be both substance to our faith and an object of our faith.

But there is a second common misunderstanding about faith. We often assume that it is a crutch for those who are hurting or are in need of some kind of transcendent intervention in a situation from which they cannot rescue themselves. How often we hear testimonies of faith from the sick and the dying or the injured and bleeding. That, we assume, is the grandest expression of faith. Without doubt, a faith that stays strong in the storms of life is a faith that must be envied.

May I suggest, however, that in reality this kind of situation is more often the realizing or the *testing* of one's faith. An equally viable faith is demonstrated when dependence upon God is shown in the midst of success, when everything is going right. That kind of faith knows that every moment and every success in life is a gift from God.

I could illustrate this in two contrasting ways. Some years ago, I had the privilege of meeting a couple by the name of Mark and Gladys Bliss, who for fourteen years were missionaries in Iran. We were together at a gathering of Iranian Christians. As the evening progressed, our Iranian host took me aside and began to tell me the Blisses' story.

In 1969, he said, Mark and Gladys were driving with their children and some friends to visit a new church some miles from Teheran. In fact, said this gentleman, "I was a young lad, and they had come to my house to pick me up for this trip. But I couldn't go." On their journey late at night, they met with a terrible accident in which all three Bliss children—thirteen-year-old Karen, eleven-year-old Debbie, and three-year-old Mark—were killed. The other couple with them in the car lost their six-month-old baby in that awful tragedy. (On a side note, it was the father of that six-month-old who, twenty-five years later, was martyred. Haik Hovsepian was stabbed to death because of his love and service for Jesus Christ. Evidently, early tragedy had not diminished his faith.)

As I heard this story, I glanced toward Mark and Gladys Bliss, and my heart sank. How was it possible to look so at peace when you have buried your three children at the tender ages of protective need? An ache such as that seems too large to contain within the heart. "Their testimony became a shining light in our community," said this Iranian man. "Only their faith in God carried them through."

Contrast this with the following. Some years ago, I was invited to the Orient by a businessman to address a gathering of people called "diamond-collared" executives. He himself is known to be one of the wealthiest men in his country. In fact, I subsequently realized that he is listed by those who make such lists as one of the ten wealthiest people in the world. When I arrived there, I asked him what had brought him to place his trust in Jesus Christ.

"Oh," he said, "about eighteen months ago, I said to my wife, 'I have everything in life, but I am still so empty. I do not know where to turn. I believe I need God.'" His wife supported that yearning. With that they began their search and found their way to Jesus Christ. Nothing dramatic. No big crusade. Just a regular attendance at a weekly Bible study group, and they were now in tune with the wealth of a newfound relationship with Jesus Christ.

Was the faith of the one any less than the faith of the other? It may be true that perhaps one has been tested more than the other. But certainly, to turn to God when all your earthly needs are already met is to express in no uncertain terms that faith in God is to trust Him even when other supports are within reach. Jesus said that for a rich man to make such a commitment was almost impossible. But thankfully He went on to say that with God it was possible.

You see, that is the way God has designed us. One of the most startling things about life is that it does not start with reason and end with faith. It starts in childhood with faith and is sustained either by reasoning through that faith or by blindly leaving the reason for faith unaddressed. The child's mind has a very limited capacity to inform it of the reason for its trust. But whether she nestles on her mother's shoulder, nurses at her mother's breast, or runs into her father's arms, she does so because of an implicit trust that those shoulders will bear her, that her food will sustain her, and that those arms will hold her. If over time that trust is tested, it will be the character of the parent that will either prove that trust wise or foolish. Faith is not bereft of reason.

FAITH AND UNREASON

There is another side. Jesus reminded His followers that the commitment of the will is a fickle thing when it comes up against the beckoning arms of God. The tendency of the human heart is so defiant that every generation will find ways to challenge that which God proclaims. This point is critical in order to understand that whatever proof is offered at any time in history, we will always demand something else. In Luke 7:31–35, Jesus said:

> To what, then, can I compare the people of this generation? What are they like? They are like children sitting in the marketplace and calling out to each other:
>
> > "We played the flute for you,
> > and you did not dance;
> > we sang a dirge,
> > and you did not cry."
>
> For John the Baptist came neither eating bread nor drinking wine, and you say, "He has a demon." The Son of Man came eating and drinking, and you say, "Here is a glutton and a drunkard, a friend of tax collectors and 'sinners.'" But wisdom is proved right by all her children.

By this Jesus powerfully exposed the bent of the human will. When John warned them of the severity of the law, they called him demon-possessed because they wanted more liberty. When Jesus came and mingled with the outcasts of society, they called Him a hedonist because they wanted a tighter reign over the law. But Jesus declared that wisdom reveals itself by what it produces. It does not take more than one look at our society to see the utter absence of wisdom, and it is because we understand neither law nor grace. To such a mind-set, faith will always be caricatured as a symptom of credulity. Jesus was not hesitant to call their bluff, as He does ours.

But He turned the tables on them and reminded them that their faithlessness to what they knew to be true said more about their own character than it did about the evidence. This, I believe, is the essential component that is often missing from a discussion of faith. Yes, there is the component of content that speaks to the truth. Yes, there is the component of love that speaks to the blending of the emotion and commitment. But there is also the component of honesty that speaks to the truthfulness or the integrity of the individual. It is here that the battle lines are publicly drawn. It is here that the real truth about reason is revealed.

THE REAL CONFLICT

A recent article in the *Times* in England titled "The Rage of Reason," penned by Matthew Parris, is fairly typical of a thinker who claims to be a lover of reason over against the irrationality of religion. He punctuates his plea with a wish for the Bertrand Russells, Thomas Paines, and David Humes of the past to return and deliver us from the scourge of the "religious nonsense" around. I cannot engage all of what he says in this space, but let me respond to at least one of his invocations.

Echoing the words of Blake in calling for Milton—"Oh Milton, thou shouldest be living at this hour, England hath need of thee!"—Parris entreats, "Oh David Hume, thou shouldest be living at this hour, we have need of thee."[3]

David Hume, who lived in the eighteenth century, was one of the most vocal philosophers to contend for the factual nature of science against what he termed the irrationality of religion. He was a thoroughgoing skeptic, and his philosophical attack upon the nature of religious belief is echoed in academic halls to this day. Hume roundly denounced the very possibility of miracles.

The writer of the *Times* article, Parris, quotes these famous lines from Hume, lines that many skeptics have repeatedly used without having pondered them carefully: "The Christian religion not only was at first attended with miracles, but even at this day cannot be believed by any reasonable person without one." So said Hume, and so far, so good.

But now note what Hume says must be the test for anything meaningful:

If we take in our hand any volume: of divinity or school of metaphysics, for instance; let us ask, *Does it contain any abstract reasoning concerning quantity or number?* No. *Does it contain any experimental reasoning concerning matter of fact and existence?* No. Commit it then to the flames; For it can contain nothing but sophistry and illusion.[4]

Quoting these lines with an air of triumph, Parris seems to think that a devastating, knockout punch has been delivered to religion so that it now lies unconscious before the stupendous stature of science. All religion has been stigmatized as nothing but "sophistry and illusion" because its "volume of divinity" does not stand the test of either mathematics or science. Unless a statement fits into either of these categories, it must be "tossed into the flames."

The only problem with Mr. Parris's test for meaning, quoting Hume, is that *the test itself does not pass the test.* David Hume's grand statement is neither scientific nor mathematical. If, in order to be meaningful, a statement must be either mathematically sustained or scientifically verifiable, then David Hume's statement itself is meaningless. It is a philosophical solvent that dissolves itself. The emperor has no clothes, while boasting the finest threads.

What unmitigated arrogance to so narrow reason when, in truth, it is this kind of unreason that has lost sight of itself! The Bible, in fact, speaks of such a person, who looks in the mirror and then walks away, forgetting what he looks like. Writers like Parris, who brag that they live in the bright sunlight of reason and wish to deliver this world from the darkness of every religious belief, abound today. They are only outwardly more sophisticated than the woman on the side of the road who said, "If you want to believe he exists, then he exists." Their hollow reasoning is no less self-serving. I dealt with this critique of Hume at Oxford University recently, and one student came at the end and said "OK, we are unreasonable, so what!" Our subsequent conversation could fit into either tragedy or comedy, depending on one's mood.

How tragic that so many are living in the darkness of unreason, clinging to their absolute skepticism. The prophecies, person, and work of Christ, His resurrection from the dead, and numerous other affirmations do have points of verification in history. What does the naturalist do with them? No, the Christian's faith is not a leap into the dark; it is a well-placed trust in the light—the Light of the World, who is Jesus.

But that is only one-half of the naturalist's problem. Some years ago, I was having dinner with a few scholars, most of whom were scientists. They were a fine group of people, and I was honored to be in their company. At one point, our discussion veered into the conflict between naturalism's starting point—nature and nature alone—and supernaturalism's starting point, which is that God is the only sufficient explanation for our origin.

I asked them a couple of questions. "If the Big Bang were indeed where it all began [which one can fairly well grant, at least to this point in science's thinking], may I ask what preceded the Big Bang?" Their answer, which I had anticipated, was that the universe was shrunk down to a singularity.

I pursued, "But isn't it correct that a singularity as defined by science is a point at which all the laws of physics break down?"

"That is correct," was the answer.

"Then, technically, your starting point is not scientific either."

There was silence, and their expressions betrayed the scurrying mental searches for an escape hatch. But I had yet another question.

I asked if they agreed that when a mechanistic view of the universe had held sway, thinkers like Hume had chided philosophers for taking the principle of causality and applying it to a philosophical argument for the existence of God. Causality, he warned, could not be extrapolated from science to philosophy.

"Now," I added, "when quantum theory holds sway, randomness in the subatomic world is made a basis for randomness in life. Are you not making the very same extrapolation that you warned us against?"

Again there was silence and then one man said with a self-deprecating smile, "We scientists do seem to retain selective sovereignty over what we allow to be transferred to philosophy and what we don't."

There is the truth in cold, hard terms. The person who demands a sign and at the same time has already determined that anything that cannot be explained scientifically is meaningless is not merely stacking the deck; he is losing at his own game.

THE MIND BEHIND THE QUESTIONER

There remains yet one thing that needs to be said about the demand for a sign. Is that demand not a sign in itself? After all, the reason a sign is demanded is because we are intelligent beings. We seek evidence because we think, and thinking cannot but be the result of a mind. But our minds cannot justify our propensity for reason if there were no ultimate reason and no mind behind the existence of our minds, because the framing of our minds is the result of complex information. We must marvel not only at what the mind seeks, but at what the mind is. Lewis Thomas makes this comment in *Medusa and the Snail* about the information-rich blueprint in the human gene.

> The mere existence of that cell should be one of the greatest astonishments of the earth. People ought to be walking around all day, all through their waking hours, calling to each other in endless wonderment, talking of nothing except that cell. . . . If anyone does succeed in explaining it, within my lifetime I will charter a skywriting airplane, maybe a whole fleet of them, and send them aloft to write one great exclamation point after another, around the whole sky, until all my money runs out.[5]

Writing about this same human cell, Chandra Wickramasinghe, professor of applied mathematics at the University of Cardiff, Wales, reminded his readers that the statistical probability of forming even a single enzyme, the building block of the gene, which is in turn the building block of the cell, is 1 in $10^{40,000}$. The translation of that figure is that it would require more attempts for the formation of one enzyme than there are atoms in all the stars of all the galaxies in the entire known universe. Though a Buddhist, Dr. Wickramasinghe concedes this supernatural notion.[6]

So "impossible" is this event that Francis Crick, the Nobel Prize–winning scientist who helped crack the code of human DNA, said it is "almost a miracle."[7]

In short, both David Hume's own test and Bertrand Russell's plea for evidence force one to wonder who has to have more faith. Is it the Christian who uses his mind to trust in God, or is it the one who, without any attempt to explain how his mind came to be, nevertheless uses that mind to demand a sign and disbelieves in God? When Russell was asked to explain the existence of the universe, he said, "It's just there." That is not an explanation. That is an explaining away. King David said long ago in his psalms of praise to God, "I am fearfully and wonderfully made" (Ps. 139:14).

Years ago, I read an episode of the cartoon strip "Born Loser." Brutus Thornapple was seen lounging beside a magnificent stretch of beach. He turned to a stranger next to him and confided, "I was able to afford this trip because of a ten-thousand-dollar insurance claim on a fire in my house."

The man replied, "I am here because of a twenty-thousand-dollar insurance claim on a flood that destroyed my house."

Brutus looked utterly defeated and then turned to face the man, whispering, "How does one start a flood?"

Little fires and little floods are easy to start if you have matches and water. How does a universe, which itself developed from nothing, impart into every human strand of DNA enough specific information to cover six hundred thousand pages of information from nothing? Intelligence is intrinsic to our makeup. Jesus warned against taking what is intrinsic and manipulating it into a scenario that excludes other equally intrinsic facets that drive us to God.

In summary, therefore, faith in Jesus Christ is a cognitive, passionate, and moral commitment to that which stands up under the scrutiny of the mind, the heart, and the conscience. It is not an escapist grasp that comes to the rescue when life is out of control. It is recasting every threat and possibility that life presents into the design of God.

This is why Jesus challenged the notion that more evidence would have generated more faith. George Macdonald said years ago that to give truth to him who does not love the truth is to only give more reasons for misinterpretation.

THE GREATEST PROOF OF ALL

Now Jesus places the *text* of His answer against the ultimate test of His claim:

"Destroy this temple, and in three days I will raise it up."

What greater proof could He offer than to rise from the dead? Naturalism is compelled to believe that death is the cessation of life, the irreversible ceasing of one's brain activity. There is a sense of finality about death that centuries of discussion have not been able to dissipate. The philosopher Albert Camus said wryly, "Death is philosophy's only problem." If somehow death could be conquered, life could be redefined.

Jesus gave the greatest proof of His authority by accurately predicting His death and the time of His bodily resurrection. Of all people, the temple authorities should have been alert to His promise, but they never dreamed that it would actually come to be. They were sure it was an empty boast. The fulfillment of that prediction reveals the uniqueness of Jesus above all contenders.

It is important to note that Jesus did not predict merely a spiritual resurrection. That would have been an easy way out. He predicted a *physical,* verifiable resurrection. After He was laid in the tomb, the temple authorities needed only to produce His body to disprove His claim. But they could not. He proved precisely what He said He would.

The hope that He brings is in the demonstration that death has been conquered. Paul, recognizing the Christian claim, said that if the hope that comes from Christ being raised from the dead is not true, "we are of all men most miserable" (1 Cor. 15:19 KJV). It was the encounter with the resurrected Jesus that turned this obstinate individual, a murderer named Saul of Tarsus, into the apostle Paul.

But the uniqueness of His resurrection is not left as a "futuristic" hope. It is tied into present privileges and responsibilities. This is where Jesus moved beyond their pretext and His text to the larger context for all of us.

WHEN BODIES DO NOT MATTER

At the beginning of this chapter, I stated that there was a reason Jesus used the concept of the body to talk about the temple. His words truly carried a double edge for both the skeptic and the religious person. The Bible says that those who heard Him say these words did not know that He was speaking of the temple of the body, which He called "the temple of God." That is the context within which He gave His answer. He lifted their sights beyond stones and mortar to the place where He seeks to dwell—within every human being. Your body and my body are His temple.

This is an extraordinary conferral of sanctity upon what it means to be human. It means that this body is deemed worthy of respect and reverence. Not only is the proof of Jesus' authority different from any other claimant to deity, its application and implication present a world of difference.

Please take very careful note of what I am saying now. In all pantheistic religions and in New Age thinking, the body is seen as an extension or continuation of the universe. Popular speaker and writer Deepak Chopra is a classic example of this. He is an exponent on the themes of spirituality, wealth, and success, and he is representative of a world-view that in essence is pantheistic and prides itself on its blend of naturalism with the spiritual. Chopra makes a case for our material commonality with every part of the universe. He further argues that, in its randomness, the subatomic world provides the basis for all of life. From this randomness and cosmic oneness we find our being, our common values, and spiritual goals. This is how he explains it in his book *The Seven Spiritual Laws of Success:*

> On the material level, both you and [a] tree are made up of the same recycled elements: mostly carbon, hydrogen, oxygen, nitrogen, and other elements in minute amounts. You could buy these elements in a hardware store for a couple of dollars. . . . The real difference between the two of you is in the energy and in the information. . . . Your body is not separate from the body of the universe, because at quantum mechanical levels there are no well-defined edges. You are like a wiggle, a wave, a fluctuation, a convolution, a whirlpool, a localized disturbance in the larger quantum field. The larger quantum field—the universe—is your extended body.[8]

One must wonder how such thinking can actually retain logical integrity. In effect, it violates the disciplines of both science and of religion. *It reduces my being to sheer matter while spiritualizing it and exalts the mind to spiritual supremacy while naturalizing it.* To base an entire philosophy of life on the impersonal subatomic world while espousing both randomness and absoluteness is to give the impression of doing magic with words. Chopra makes philosophical extrapolations that are quantum leaps in themselves. One might as well argue that if his deductions are true, his philosophizing is nothing more than a wiggle or a wave or a localized disturbance. Such is the seduction and reduction of this kind of thinking, supposedly done in the name of wisdom and success. Chopra's world of human essence and Jesus' description of human worth are at opposite poles.

A truth gleaned from Shakespeare's *The Merchant of Venice* provides an illustration here. This is basically the story of a man who had loaned some money to the friend of a friend. The moneylender, Shylock, held his friend, Antonio, responsible for the debt until it was repaid. If the debt was not repaid, according to the deal, Shylock was owed a pound of flesh from Antonio's side. Predictably, Antonio's ships were lost at sea, and when the debt became due, he did not have the wherewithal to pay Shylock. With glee, Shylock demanded his pound of flesh, as was his due according to the law. But the judge, not to be outdone, declared, "You can have your pound of flesh, but if even one drop of blood is spilled in the process, you will have to pay with your own blood." All of a sudden, Shylock had lost at his own game.

It is no more possible to take a pound of live flesh without the shedding of blood than it is possible to make the body inviolable while reducing it to sheer matter. Naturalists cannot have their pound of flesh without bleeding the life out of it. Through the substance of human flesh flows life. Life is more than matter. Religions that attempt to keep the body sacred while denying the Creator's hand are in the same boat as skeptics who try to protect life while saying it is nothing more than matter.

All the desacralizing that has engulfed our culture lies in this very struggle to understand the place and sacredness of the body. The right of every individual life, even the one still in its mother's womb; the pleasure and consummation of sexual delights, reserved for the sanctity of marriage; the injunction against suicide; the care and protection of one's health; the injunction against killing; and the command to love others more than we love ourselves and to work for their good—all of these flow from the fact that this body becomes the dwelling place of God. Our world would be a different place if we comprehended this sobering privilege.

Having lost this truth, what are we left with? Pornography and the cruel degradation of men, women, and children; death in the womb in the name of personal rights; the breakdown of the family for myriad reasons; the profanation of sex in our entertainment industry; violence in unprecedented proportions. One can only weep for the bleeding and the loss. In losing the high value that God has placed on the body, we are in a free fall, at the mercy of greed, cruelty, and lust.

During my travels in one particular part of the world, I found myself sitting next to a woman who worked for an international agency that cared for children. As we talked, she confessed to me that after all she had seen in her work, it was very difficult to remain optimistic about the future of this world. Why, I asked her, had she become so cynical? She paused and began a narration of heartbreaking stories. She named a particular city where she had been recently and described the horror of all that went on there. In a section in that city called "Snake Alley," men come at night and drink a combination of snake's blood and alcohol. When they are under its influence, they are taken into a back room where children are offered to them for their sexual pleasure. This woman told me that the youngest one they rescued from this terrible state was only eleven months old. Many, of course, are used this way and then killed, often in the act itself. "Where are the city fathers of a city such as that?" I asked. "They are on the take," was her sad reply.

How is it possible for something like that to be given legitimacy? Or is it just easier to pretend it does not happen? The scourge of violence and vileness is the offspring of a mind that has lost respect for the body while the body has lost its sanctity.

Nearer home, though the stories are different, the rationale is the same. In March 1998, two boys ages eleven and thirteen went on a shooting rampage in their school in Jonesboro, Arkansas, killing four girls and a teacher and injuring ten others. That tragedy at Westside Middle School was at the time the largest school massacre in America. On the night of the shootings, many were being counseled in small groups in the hospital waiting room. Friends and relatives were waiting for word of the victims. The whole scene was one of desolation and horror.

In one corner sat a woman alone, looking dazed and helpless. A counselor went to her to see if she needed any assistance and discovered that she was the mother of one of the girls who had been killed. She had no husband, no friends, and no family. "I just came to find out how to get my little girl's body back," she said. But the body had been taken to Little Rock, one hundred miles away, for an autopsy.[9]

"I just came to get my little girl's body back."

She did not come to pick up a wiggle or a wave or a fluctuation. She came to pick up the body of her daughter, not just an extension of the universe. What a grim reminder that is to the rest of us. We trivialize the body in our indulgences. We treat it as a means to other ends. But when death comes, we grasp at it and cling to it because it is all we have left.

Jesus made it clear that the body is not just informationally different from other quantities; it is purposefully different. That is why the resurrection is a physical one at its core. The body matters in the eternal sense, not just the temporal.

A REMARKABLE COMPLIMENT

The final ramification of Jesus' words to all of us is gratifying, for if our bodies are His dwelling place, worship rises above a location. In no other religious world-view is this connection made between the body and the temple. In fact, in every other world-view the body is distinct from the temple. Rules are laid out for the body before it can enter the temple. A litany of prerequisites surrounds entry into so-called "holy places" of worship.

During the course of writing this book, I had the privilege of witnessing in one country a festival called Thaipusam. As I walked in the midst of teeming masses and saw all that was going on in a desire to worship, my mind was in a constant state of shock. Devotees involved in this ceremony demonstrate the terrifying extent to which they are willing to go in order to gain the favor of their god. Iron spears are pierced into their bodies, and large skewers are forced from one side of their faces through to the other. Another skewer is pierced through their tongues, and the devotees parade for miles and for hours with this apparatus on them. In fact, trailing each one is a helper, who holds reins on the hooks and pulls in the opposite direction, compelling the devotee to strain against the force as he walks the long trek. At the end of the journey, he mounts one hundred steps to the temple of Lord Murugan, the second son of the Hindu god, Shiva.

One is surprised to see that the flesh does not rip and the blood flow is minimal, if any. Each devotee is in a trance. The temple is busy as each participant arrives and is unhooked from the weight he has been laboring under, and the ceremony continues. The ashen mark on his forehead at the end of the day is ash from burned and "purified" cow dung. All this is to win the blessing of the one he worships in the "sanctity" of the temple, *the place of encounter with his god,* and to be blessed at the hands of the priest. How did such strange beliefs come to pass?

Readers will remember the assassination of India's prime minister, Indira Gandhi. The murder was prompted by revenge because she had sent the military into the Sikh Temple, where weapons were being stored. She was murdered in order to preserve a temple. Jesus would have told them that they had actually destroyed what was intended to be His temple in order to preserve a place.

More recently, Hindus and Muslims engaged in bombings and killings over the sacred birthplace of a Hindu deity, upon which a mosque had been built. This anger, ironically, is the logical outworking of a belief that exalts places into exclusive venues where God is met or encountered. Muslims will never allow a church in their country to have a steeple taller than a mosque. In fact, where there is already an existing church, it is not uncommon for Muslims to build a mosque next to it that is taller.

Islam ridicules Christianity for profaning God's name, calling Jesus' incarnation blasphemous. But in His incarnation He exalts the body, first by being conceived in the womb of a virgin, then by taking on human form and giving it the glorious expression of God in the flesh.

The history of Christendom is not free from perversions. But Jesus sent a message loud and clear. *We* are His temple. We do not turn in a certain direction to pray. We are not bound by having to go into a building so that we can commune with God. There are no unique postures and times and limitations that restrict our access to God. My relationship with God is intimate and personal. The Christian does not go to the temple to worship. The Christian takes the temple with him or her. Jesus lifts us beyond the building and pays the human body the highest compliment by making it His dwelling place, the place where He meets with us. Even today He would overturn the tables of those who make it a marketplace for their own lust, greed, and wealth.

Was this not the stunning truth behind the woman's expression as she poured the alabaster ointment on Jesus, as described in Luke 7? On one hand it was to prepare for His death, but on the other hand something greater had taken place. She was a woman of ill repute. Her life's living was possibly earned through prostitution. Now Jesus welcomed her and restored the worth of the human body to her. In her soiled earthly temple, she came to give an offering to Him whose dwelling place it would be. Jesus said of her that wherever the gospel story would be told, the story of what this woman had done for Him would also be told. It was the ultimate transaction between her corruption and His purity. It represented the changed relationship between the dwelling and its occupant. "Christ in you," said the apostle Paul, is "the hope of glory" (Col. 1:27). What more glorious news than to find out that He seeks to live within you?

"What sign do You give us?" they cried.

"Destroy this body and in three days I will raise it up."

They did not know He spoke of the temple of the body. Why? Because in their greed and love of power, they were focused on a temple made of stone. How much they lost in exploiting other people, other temples—and indeed themselves—within which God wanted to dwell. No other claimant would have answered it Jesus' way.

Chapter Four

A Taste for the Soul

"Truth is stranger than fiction," it is said.

G. K. Chesterton, with his ever-ready wit, told us why that is so: "It is because we have made fiction to suit ourselves." Modern-day techniques have only enhanced the capacity to mass-produce lies. With that combination of propensity and facility, we live with the reality that sometimes the truth seems impossible to believe.

Some years ago, my family and I were visiting the city of Bedford, England, a little west of where we were living in Cambridge. In the heart of Bedford stands a larger-than-life statue of the famed seventeenth-century author John Bunyan. In fact, so imposing is the size of that sculpture that some prankster has painted bold, gigantic white footsteps from the edifice all the way to the public toilets. The message implied, sarcastically or otherwise, is that Bunyan still lives.

Any reader of literature knows that though Bunyan has long been dead, his brilliant work, *Pilgrim's Progress,* does indeed live on. That book has been translated into more languages than any other book in history, with the exception of the Bible. We wandered through the museum built to his memory, where there was exhibited a copy of the book in every language in which it has been printed. We were quite impressed by the people of various nationalities engrossed in the display, walking from room to room, studying the exhibits.

As I was leaving, I commented to the woman at the front desk, "Isn't it amazing that a simple little book from the hands of a mender of pots and pans has won such worldwide acclaim?"

She paused and said, "I suppose that is true, but I must confess that I haven't read it."

If there hadn't been a hard floor beneath me, I would have voluntarily fainted. Unable to help myself, I asked her, "Why not?"

"I found it too difficult, I suppose," came the very dispassionate reply.

If shock were to be measured along a scale, at this point, I was nearly off the chart. What does one say to the person who sells tickets to a museum, the existence of which is owed to one book, while she herself has left the work unread? I recommended that for the sake of sheer curiosity, if not propriety, she might at least try the children's version so she could get a mild taste of what the interest was all about.

What a remarkable illustration of self-inflicted poverty! It is possible to hold a treasure in your hand but be ignorant of it and go for the wrapping instead. This proximity to truth and distance from its worth is repeated innumerable times in our lives. In Chesterton's words, we hold the dust and let the gold go free.

No one saw this tragedy lived out more than Jesus did. The masses came to Him frequently and left embracing lesser things while forfeiting the real treasure He was offering them. He often expressed surprise at their shallowness in being unable to look beyond the surface.

One of the most dramatic illustrations of this failing was illustrated in their encounter with a truth at once so captivating and so dramatic. The lingering tragedy throughout history is that millions have made the same mistake and left these words of Jesus either unread or shamefully distorted.

I faced its implication once in a public challenge. I had just finished a talk before a somewhat hostile audience in India. During the question-and-answer time, a man abruptly shouted from the back of the tent, "Christians are cannibals! Jesus promoted cannibalism!"

There was absolutely no logical or thematic connection between what I had spoken on and his outburst. His attack only revealed his animosity toward the message of the Christian faith. In my experience, while I never get used to such attacks, I certainly have learned to anticipate them. The natural inclination is to fight back and to dish out exactly what you are facing—derision for derision, blow for blow, gibe for gibe.

But that is not the answer to an angry questioner. In fact, such a response would only diminish the effectiveness of any answer. The truth is that as I stood there, I had a fairly good idea why this man was insinuating what he did, although most of the audience gasped at his assertion.

My response was a simple counter. "Why do you say that, and what is your source?"

He had none. He assured me that if I gave him time to run back to his home and check the book in which he had read it he could sustain his charge.

He really did not need to go searching for his book. I could have pretty much named the philosopher he had read and on what page he had made that allegation. Antitheistic philosophers have not spared their scorn in their eagerness to mock this, of all Jesus' sayings. So I knew precisely what this student had in mind. I did offer him the platform to come up and debate the point, but he turned down the offer.

"Christians are cannibals!"

What on earth was he talking about? Had he ever read the Bible? Did he ever seek an explanation for what he read? Or was this the way he wanted it to read?

For those who have grown up in a Christian home or who have been raised with an active church life such a bizarre thought may have never been entertained. But for one who comes to Christ from outside a Christian environment, or for the skeptic in search of an argument, a particular passage does leap out of the Scriptures with discomforting coarseness. The words are unadorned to impress sensitivities.

"This is My body. . . . Take and eat." "This is My blood. . . . Drink all of it."

These words of Jesus prompted such shock when He spoke them that I cannot completely fault the student for his reaction. I well remember as a young lad hearing those poignant lines intoned in a ministerial pitch, Sunday after Sunday, at the church to which I was reluctantly dragged. But what I recall most is that I dreaded the length of the service and had no idea what those words portended—in fact, I never even gave them a thought. I did see people walking up the aisle, kneeling at the altar with palms cupped, receiving something that they would put into their mouths. For my part, I had it all timed. I knew that when those words were uttered we were about twenty minutes away from the end of the service, and I was an hour away from being on the cricket field or in the movie theater.

I was so close to one of the most sublime truths and transactions ever taught and demonstrated by Jesus, yet I was oblivious to its meaning. Like the clerk at Bunyan's home, I had left those words unread. Now I know that for someone who truly seeks to understand what all this means, its depth is immeasurable.

Once again, if we are to follow the path to understanding we must lay hold of the sequence to Jesus' assertions. First, the simple, then, the profound. His utterance, I believe, offers an element of the gospel that stands in brilliant and unarguably unique contrast to other faiths.

PROPELLED BY THE SENSATIONAL

> Earth's crammed with heaven,
> And every common bush afire with God;
> But only he who sees takes off his shoes;
> The rest sit round it and pluck blackberries.[1]

So said the poet Elizabeth Barrett Browning. Her lament takes us back to that spellbinding encounter when God appeared to Moses in the burning bush and issued a call to him that he might lead His people out of slavery into a land flowing with milk and honey. That epiphany, as Browning points out, was not for Moses' culinary delight. No more, I might add, than the thunder and lightning on Sinai were so that the people could enjoy the glow on the landscape.

The dazzling, almost fearsome accompaniment of the elements in both these defining moments for His people pointed beyond the portents to the One who controlled those elements. God's inexhaustible presence graced those occasions with brilliant and awesome splendor. How inconceivable was the loss for the people when the signs became the ends in themselves and the One signified became the means. The special effects became the attraction, and the central figure was obscured. The world of humanity has lived with such blindness, and the mistake has been repeated in virtually every life.

And so it was that, centuries after the event, people were still locked into that blindness. The crowd in Jesus' ministry followed Him and intruded upon His time alone. They came with a one-upmanship challenge to Him to match the manna from heaven that Moses gave his people. They were not expecting an answer anywhere near as jarring as His. Talking about bread was the easier part. What followed was staggering to them. By the time He had finished, many left Him, asking, "How can we accept such a hard saying?"

The truth, in this instance, *was* beyond belief because the mind was unwilling to ponder the provision and, of course, the implication. Between their expectation and His offer was a wide chasm, and they started to leave without seeking an explanation. Jesus then looked at His disciples and asked if they were going to leave Him too. Was this all too much for them to comprehend?

After His death, they would relive those moments and remember what He had said. Millennia later, while the Church repeats those words in virtually every language, many have found the teaching too difficult and still leave these words unstudied.

Misreading the Script

When Jesus said, "Take and eat; this is my body. . . . Drink from it, all of you. This is my blood of the covenant" (Matt. 26:26–28), He was not speaking in a cultural vacuum to consign His followers to cannibalism. Rather, His words were intended to lift the listeners from their barren, food-dominated existence to the recognition of the supreme hunger of life that could only be filled by different bread. It was in that very journey under Moses that He had first told them that physical bread had limited sustenance. He wanted to meet a greater hunger.

To a culture with such specific instruction on their spiritual need, to say nothing of their strict dietary laws, only ignorance would manufacture the notion that Jesus was prescribing the consumption of human flesh. Their charge that it was "a hard saying" betrayed a serious misunderstanding. It is just that response that leaves every human being bereft of life's real meaning.

The longer I have pondered these words, the more profoundly I am moved to realize why our hunger for something transcendent is so rooted in our very being, yes, even in our physical craving. That may be why we cannot shrug it off, however hard we try.

It is, therefore, a significant loss that a teaching so great has been met with an understanding so shallow. Unfortunately, like the questioning student in India, rather than getting to the truth that Jesus is revealing, many "sit round it" instead, as philosophers or critics, and "eat blackberries."

What is the context we have? What preceded this demand by the crowd to bring down food from heaven?

Before his record of this conversation, John had already described several miracles that Jesus had done. The first was the conversion of water into wine, in which Jesus revealed His power over the elements. Then John narrated two episodes of healing, in which Jesus showed His power over sickness. Following that, he relates Jesus' multiplication of a young lad's lunch to feed five thousand people—His power over all provision. Finally, he pens the well-known story of Jesus walking on water—His power over natural law.

An incredible history of response has followed these stories, ranging from the reverential to the ridiculous, from the artistic to the philosophical. Capturing the beauty of the conversion of the water into wine, the poet Alexander Pope said, "The conscious water saw its Master and blushed." That sublime description could be reworked to explain each one of these miracles. Was it any different in principle for a broken body to mend at the command of its Maker? Was it far-fetched for the Creator of the universe, who fashioned matter out of nothing, to multiply bread for the crowd? Was it not within the power of the One who called all the molecules into existence to interlock them that they might bear His footsteps? Why were they not making that connection?

But is this not the very impertinence that grasps the gift and ignores the giver? Naturalism by its purpose engineers the displacement of the miracle and puts in its place explanations that defy reason. Those who smirk at His walking on water have forgotten the miracle He has already performed in the very composition of water.

Think of this for a moment. In eighteen milliliters of water (about two swallows full), there are 6×10^{23} molecules of H_2O. How much is 6×10^{23}? A good computer can carry out ten million counts per second. It would take that computer two billion years to count to 6×10^{23}.

Look at it another way. A stack of five hundred sheets of paper is two to three inches high. How high would the stack be if it had 6×10^{23} sheets? That stack would reach from the earth to the sun, not once, but more than one million times.[2]

Yet, in about two gulps of water, God has packed that many molecules. The miracle of walking on water is small for Him who created it in the first place. The multiplication of bread was but a simple command for Him when the very earth was brought forth at His command. (C. S. Lewis commented that a slow miracle is no easier to perform than an instant one.) The skeptic, of course, will challenge such credulity that accepts wholesale such stories, not realizing that what they swallow in a glass of water is a miracle in and of itself!

The people and the disciples who saw Jesus performing the miracle of feeding the multitude followed Him with deliberate intentions. They sought the very power that they assumed would make life more delectable—to ensure a full stomach and a limitless supply of bread. Who could fault them? I heard recently of a man who had won an enormous sum in a lottery. "What is the biggest difference in your life?" asked an interviewer. "I eat out more often," came the matter-of-fact answer.

Food and power distracted the mind from the need of nourishment for the soul. The generosity of God, incidental to the miracles, became a stumbling block because the eyewitnesses lost sight of the purpose of the deed and longed only to replicate the capacity in themselves. They wanted to know how a little boy's lunch could feed several thousand people and still have baskets full of crumbs left over. How could a paralytic of nearly four decades suddenly walk again? Is this power transferable? Can it be bought?

It is crucial to note that Jesus' response to their demand is in stark contrast to the self-aggrandizement that would-be messiahs covet. Rather than bask in the accolades of a feigning crowd and soak in their praise or enlarge His following, Jesus slipped away from their clamoring midst. In fact, He wept over their self-deception. He knew the motives and the misconceptions with which they lived. And when they somehow tracked Him down, they burst upon Him with a question, "Our fathers ate manna in the desert. . . . Why don't You give us the same?"

This is where He began His answer that was to lead them farther than they had ever planned on going. But He first tried to lead them away from their error before He could bring them to His truth.

IGNORING THE AUTHOR

It is not surprising that the first temptation Jesus faced in the wilderness was to change stones into bread. "Do this," said Satan, "and the world will follow You."

Anyone who has been in countries where hunger is publicly exposed as a means for eliciting pity and a handout can easily understand the emotional tug of such a temptation. I myself was raised in a land where there was never a shortage of hungry people. How can food sit comfortably in your stomach when someone else's hurts for the lack of it? This was, therefore, not a soft temptation thrust upon Jesus. The tempter knew, precisely, the force of his taunt. How much more relevant could God be than to be a provider of food for life? What good is religion if it cannot feed the hungry? Satan was perilously and painfully close to a truth. But it was a half-truth, and a half-truth gets so interwoven with a lie that it becomes deadlier by the mix.

Ask yourself this question: What kind of a following would result if the sole reason for the affection toward the leader is that he provides his followers with bread? Both motives would be wrong—for the provider and the receiver. These are the terms of reward and punishment that are mercenarily tainted and have diminishing returns, at best engendering compliance, but not love. Their appeal, too, is soon lost when offered as enticements or when withheld to engender fears. Dependence without commitment will ever look for ways to break the stranglehold.

The temptation Satan posed to Jesus stalked Him throughout His ministry, even as the crowd was increasing with their demand for a limitless supply of bread. Politics of power through abundance is not a new invention.

That is the way demagogues have controlled the masses. Jesus took pains to show them that their preoccupation with bread as the primary purpose and expression of enjoyment of life had seriously displaced both what bread was meant to do and what life was meant to be.

In our high-paced living, this truth does not sink in with any greater ease than it did in ancient Palestine. With all our ingesting and consumption, our hungers are still many and our fulfillments are few. Must we not think about that? Is that not in itself an indicator that our hungers are displaced?

In his play *Our Town,* Thornton Wilder tells the story of life as it is lived out in the mundane and amid the hassles of daily living. The details are specific, but the lesson is like a mirror held out to all of us. We see the routine in all its monotony—the milk arrives, breakfast is eaten, working people go to their jobs, homemakers tidy their homes, handymen work in the yards— each day reflecting the previous one. In the story, the turning point comes when Emily Gibbs, in her youthful prime, dies giving birth to her baby, and the routine is suddenly broken.

From the realm of the dead, Emily was given a chance to return to earth for a day of her choice as it was actually lived out when she was on earth. Only now, from her otherworldly existence, she viewed it with nostalgic eyes. She watched the harried activity and busyness in celebration of her twelfth birthday. As she well remembered, the household was preoccupied with presents and food and chatter. The party buzzed with activity.

But now in this irreversible state, Emily noticed the complete loss of any personal attention, though her heart craved it. The focus, instead, was on the things that needed to be done, rather than the people for whom it was done. She was aghast at such blindness to all of their real needs. From the unseen, she pleaded, "Just for a moment we're happy. Let's look at one another." But her plaintive cry was unheeded. They could not hear her because they were trapped by the superficial. The party had to go on, another birthday would come, and the moments dissipated into activity. As she bid her final farewell, she cried, "Oh, Earth, you're too wonderful for anyone to realize you!"

Then she turns to the stage manager, who serves as the narrator, and asks this remorse-filled question: "Do any human beings ever realize life while they live it—every, every moment?"

The answer comes, "No. The saints and poets, maybe—they do some."

"Do any human beings ever realize life while they live it?" The only way one can realize life while one lives it is if he or she realizes that life is not a matter of nutrition alone but of the greater hunger that is beyond words and food. We do not live so that we can eat, nor do we just eat so that we can live. Life is worth living in and of itself. Life cannot be satisfied when it is lived out as a consuming entity. When it is filled by that which satisfies a hunger that is both physical *and* spiritual in a mutuality that sustains both without violation of either, only then can life be truly fulfilling. Authenticity and continuity are the offspring of the true and the eternal. For the millions who live out their lives day to day with the pursuit of bread dominating their dreams and actions, life, as it was meant to be, passes them by, and their unsatisfied hungers continue to scream out at them.

"The saints and poets, maybe—they do some," because they slow down and think and look beyond the activities to their longings and somehow broach the possibility of meaning that transcends their actions. In short, if we are to truly understand who we are, we must understand what bread can and cannot do.

Jesus has a similarly striking question for His audience, as He does for all of us. Does any one of us live every minute of life, knowing its essential worth? To realize the full impact of Jesus' patience with them, we must remember that this was not the first time the topic of food and hunger had surfaced in a conversation between Jesus and His followers. He had previously tried to bring this point home in an effort to thwart this "religion-for-bread" pursuit.

The most extended discussion had actually taken place a while before in an event that surprised the disciples—a conversation with a Samaritan woman (see John 4:1–42). In that dialogue, Jesus had tried to open up the understanding of their minds to what made up the form of life and what constituted its substance. In fact, He had a brilliant lead-in, had they but listened. Evidently the disciples missed His point.

They had their lunchbags in their hands and so were completely preoccupied. He was talking to a socially ostracized and desperate woman whose life had been used and abused till she had no sense of self-worth left. They chided Him for talking to this outcast. "You must be hungry," they said. "Is it not time to eat?"

"I have food to eat that you know nothing about. My food is to do the will of My Father."

There is the first remarkable pointer. If I am to be fulfilled, I must pursue a will that is greater than mine—a fulfilled life is one that has the will of God as its focus, not the appetite of the flesh.

He went on to say: "Open your eyes and look at the fields! They are ripe for harvest" (see John 4:32–35).

Here is our next clue. Maintaining the metaphor of food, He pointed to a hunger that was universal and that went beyond bread and water—a distinctive hunger of universal proportion. Every sentence of His response had food in it, but of a different kind. There was hunger everywhere, He said, and food enough for all. But it was not wheat or water. It was Christ Himself, the Bread of Life and the spring of living water. The Samaritan woman grasped what He said with a fervor that came from an awareness of her real need.

The transaction was fascinating. She had come with a bucket. He sent her back with a spring of living water.

She had come as a reject. He sent her back being accepted by God Himself.

She came wounded. He sent her back whole.

She came laden with questions. He sent her back as a source for answers.

She came living a life of quiet desperation. She ran back overflowing with hope.

The disciples missed it all. It was lunchtime for them.

Interestingly enough, it was only a short while after this conversation with the Samaritan woman that Jesus performed the miracle of feeding the thousands. So bread and food were not absent from His mind. He was moving them from the more difficult to the easier to perform; from the eternal to the temporal; from the soul's need to the body's hunger. But they were stuck on their desire for more food. They did not get it the first time around.

Raising the Curtain

So here it comes again in the sixth chapter of John. But this time Jesus added a very dramatic element. Hunger now takes on a wider scope, as it eventually had to if it were to be indicative of life.

If we were to enumerate all our hungers, we might be surprised at how many legitimate hungers there are. The hunger for truth, the hunger for love, the hunger for knowledge, the hunger to belong, the hunger to express, the hunger for justice, the hunger of the imagination, the hunger of the mind, and the hunger for significance. We could name more. Vast psychological theories have emerged in recognition of these hungers, or needs.

Here is the point. Some of our individual pursuits may meet some of these hungers. Education may bring knowledge. Romance may bring a sense of belonging. Accomplishments may bring significance. Wealth brings some things within reach. The message of Jesus affirms that no one thing will meet *all* of these hungers. And furthermore, none can help us know whether the way we fulfill them is legitimate or illegitimate until we feed on the bread of life that Jesus offers. That nourishment defines the legitimacy of all else.

Not only do we remain unfulfilled when we pursue these hungers, but in their very pursuit comes a disorientation that misrepresents and misunderstands where the real satisfaction comes from. This is very, very important to know.

As I mentioned previously, Jon Krakauer's book *Into Thin Air* relates the hazards that plagued the climbers in their expedition to Mount Everest during the spring of 1996. That year, the attempt to reach the summit resulted in a great loss of life. Some circumstances were out of their control, but fundamental mistakes cost them dearly. And some of those were unfortunately made while still within reach of solutions.

One of those whose life was lost was Andy Harris, one of the expedition leaders. Harris had stayed at the peak past the deadline that the leaders themselves had set. On his descent, he became in dire need of oxygen. Harris radioed his predicament to the base camp, telling them of his need and that he had come upon a cache of oxygen canisters left by other climbers, all empty. Those who had already passed by the canisters on their own return from the summit knew that they were not empty, but full. Even as they pleaded with him on the radio to make use of them, it was to no avail. Already starved for oxygen, Harris continued to argue that the canisters were empty.[3]

The problem was that the lack of what he needed so disoriented his mind that though he was surrounded by a restoring supply he continued to complain of its absence. The very thing he held in his hand was absent in his brain and ravaged his capacity to recognize what he was clutching in his grasp.

What oxygen is to the body, the Bread of Life is to the soul. Without that bread, all other hungers will be improperly perceived. In fact, in like manner, the absence of that bread over a prolonged period makes the bread itself seem worthless. Life is meant to be lived with the fulfillment of the one need that defines all other means of fulfillment and the one love that defines all other loves.

By His miracles, Jesus demonstrated from the greater to the lesser. In His answers, He moved them from the lesser to the greater. He reminded them in His words of Communion that the physical and the spiritual meet. Here the now and the forever converge. Here life and death co-mingle. Implicit in these verses is the climactic direction toward which Jesus was headed and to which He was to come back, moments before His death.

The people ought to have grasped more than they did. You see, to the Middle Eastern mind-set, bread is not just a source of nourishment. It is the bearer of so much more. Food is the means of fellowship. Jesus says, in Revelation 3:20, that He stands at the door and knocks; if anyone opens that door, He will come in and eat with him. What a beautiful expression that is of friendship. Food is the means of celebration. The return of the prodigal was celebrated by the killing of the fatted calf, which signaled that the feast had begun. Food is also a medium of pleasure. Solomon's palace thrived on such offerings. To this day, food is a big thing in eastern culture. As well as providing nourishment, it is the means of friendship, celebration, and pleasure.

We are not much different, East or West, and we know this. Yet, with all our nurture and friendships, our celebrations and pleasures, there come those crossroad moments in our lives when no food can sustain life, no friendship can overcome certain eventualities, no celebration can be endless, and no pleasure can be perfect. The body ages and weakens, and it is not within the capacity of food to ultimately restore the strength or lost youth. It moves inexorably toward a diminishing return. In short, there are two built-in limitations with food. The first is obvious. The body weakens and someday dies.

I have a friend whose life has enriched mine over the years. There came a time when his wife was stricken with cancer. I will never forget his example to me. The one word that comes to my mind is how he *cherished* her. By nature he is a busy, high-paced individual. One could get tired just watching him. Yet, when he knew her days were numbered, he dropped everything else to attend to her needs.

During the weeks and months, life ground down to one purpose, taking care of the one he loved. He sat by her side, loving her in the midst of her dissipating life. Nothing was good enough for her but fresh juices from only organically grown vegetables, processed only through a certain type of juicer. No country was too far to go to find a cure. No expense was too great to bring back her health.

But the end did finally come when her body was too far gone for any nourishment to sustain her. No bond was strong enough to hold on to her permanently. The problem was not with the nourishment or with the absence of his desire to prolong her life. The problem was that a destructive cell had so taken over her body that the best of nourishment could not restore to life what was dying.

That break comes for all of us, at different times and in different ways. The nourishment of food, the bonds of friendship, the occasions for celebration, and the delights of legitimate pleasure end in a matter of a moment for each life and each relationship.

It is to this vulnerability of living that Jesus points His finger. The poet puts it in these words:

Our life contains a thousand springs
and dies if one be gone;
Strange that a harp of a thousand strings
can stay in tune so long.

There is an old adage that says you can give a hungry man a fish, or better still, you can teach him how to fish. Jesus would add that you can teach a person how to fish, but the most successful fisherman has hungers fish will not satisfy.

GETTING BEHIND THE SCENES

There is a second but not so obvious truth. "I am the Bread of Life," said Jesus. "He who comes to Me will never go hungry, and he who believes in Me will never be thirsty." Notice the power implicit in the claim.

At the heart of every major religion is a leading exponent. As the exposition is studied, something very significant emerges. There comes a bifurcation, or a distinction, between the person and the teaching. Mohammed, to the Koran. Buddha, to the Noble Path. Krishna, to his philosophizing. Zoroaster, to his ethics.

Whatever we may make of their claims, one reality is inescapable. They are teachers who point to their teaching or show some particular way. In all of these, there emerges an instruction, a way of living. It is not Zoroaster to whom you turn. It is Zoroaster to whom you *listen*. It is not Buddha who delivers you; it is his Noble Truths that instruct you. It is not Mohammed who transforms you; it is the beauty of the Koran that woos you.

By contrast, Jesus did not only teach or expound His message. *He was identical with His message.* "In Him," say the Scriptures, "dwelt the fullness of the Godhead bodily." He did not just proclaim the truth. He said, "I *am* the truth." He did not just show a way. He said, "I *am* the Way." He did not just open up vistas. He said, "I *am* the door." "I *am* the Good Shepherd." "I *am* the resurrection and the life." "I *am* the I AM."

In Him is not just an offer of life's bread. He *is* the bread. That is why being a Christian is not just a way of feeding and living. Following Christ begins with a way of relating and being.

Let us use Buddhism as a specific example. It is a system that is gaining a following among many in Hollywood. It is often very simplistically defined as a religion of compassion and ethics. The truth is that there is probably no system of belief more complex than Buddhism. While it starts off with the four noble truths on suffering and its cessation, it then moves to the eight-fold path on how to end suffering. But as one enters the eightfold path, there emerge hundreds upon hundreds of other rules to deal with contingencies.

From a simple base of four offenses that result in a loss of one's discipleship status is built an incredible edifice of ways to restoration. Those who follow Buddha's teachings are given thirty rules on how to ward off those pitfalls. But before one even deals with those, there are ninety-two rules that apply to just one of the offenses. There are seventy-five rules for those entering the order. There are rules of discipline to be applied—two hundred and twenty-seven for men, three hundred and eleven for women. (Readers of Buddhism know that Buddha had to be persuaded before women were even permitted into a disciple's status. After much pleading and cajoling by one of his disciples, he finally acceded to the request but laid down extra rules for them.)

Whatever one may make of all of this, we must be clear that in a non-theistic system, which Buddhism is, ethics become central and rules are added ad infinitum. Buddha and his followers are the originators of these rules. The most common prayer for forgiveness in Buddhism, from the Buddhist Common Prayer, reflects this numerical maze:

I beg leave! I beg leave, I beg leave. . . . May I be freed at all times from the four states of Woe, the Three Scourges, the Eight Wrong Circumstances, the Five Enemies, the Four Deficiencies, the Five Misfortunes, and quickly attain the Path, the Fruition, and the Noble Law of Nirvana, Lord.[4]

Teaching at best beckons us to morality, but it is not in itself efficacious. Teaching is like a mirror. It can show you if your face is dirty, but the mirror will not wash your face. To truly understand this complicated theory, one would almost need a graduate-level understanding in philosophy and psychology.

By contrast, in a very simple way Jesus drew the real need of His audience to that hunger which is spiritual in nature, a hunger that is shared by every human, so that we are not human livings or human doings but human *beings*. We are not in need merely of a superior ethic, we are in need of a transformed heart and will that seek to do the will of God.

Jesus also taught and held up a mirror, but by His person He transforms our will to seek His. It is our being that Jesus wants to feed. Christ warns that there are depths to our hungers that the physical does not plumb. There are heights to existential aspirations that our activities cannot attain. There are breadths of need that the natural cannot span.

In summary, He reminds us that bread cannot sustain interminably. He is the Bread of Life that eternally sustains. And He does it as no other has ever done.

Explaining the Plot

Having made His point of the limitations of bread and that He was the eternal Bread of Life, Jesus now comes to the thought that they needed to carefully consider. No one will deny the uniqueness of the thought here. There is nothing in any other religion that would even come close to this profound teaching.

Our greatest hunger, as Jesus described it, is for a consummate relationship that combines the physical and the spiritual, that engenders both awe and love, and that is expressed in celebration and commitment.

In other words, that hunger is for worship. But worship is not accomplished only by a transaction uttered in a prayer or a wish. *Worship is a posture of life that takes as its primary purpose the understanding of what it really means to love and revere God.* It is the most sacred intimacy of all. This is where the broken piece of bread provides the means of expression and transaction.

On my first visit to the kingdom of Jordan, my family and I were hosted to a very special meal on the eve of our departure. They called it Mensef. The guests stood around a large platter of rice, beautifully garnished with succulent delicacies, flavored with aromatic spices and a gravy that gave it a mouth-watering taste. But then came the fun part. We all rolled up our sleeves and together enjoyed the meal directly from the tray, eating it with our bare hands. That was Middle Eastern food with all of its purposes and at its best. For one of Indian descent, which is my birthright, it was like coming home and more.

There is a symbolism to that way of eating. The enjoyment of a delightful combination of food, the fellowship one with the other, the touch of the hand into the same platter, the celebration of life and its purpose—all signifying trust and closeness and the memories of days we had spent together. Every detail was an invitation, saying, "Welcome to our home and become one of us." We were greeted with a kiss and bidden good-bye with a kiss. We had gathered as friends and left with an intimate trust of a deeper friendship.

That, may I add, is only an inkling of what Jesus was offering to His followers—communion with Him. Even atheistic religions like Buddhism and pantheistic religions like Hinduism, though they deny a personal, absolute God, still smuggle in ways of worship in which a personal being is addressed, only because the isolation within drives the self to a transcendent personal other.

The reason for this is that we are more than just in search of ritual. We are, in fact, broken. We have broken away from God; we are broken in relation to our fellow human beings. And the most elusive reality is that we are broken even from ourselves. We do not connect our own proclivities. Life is a story of brokenness.

This is at the core of the gospel. We have come apart from within. And to this brokenness, Jesus brings the real answer, not just a simplistic "come and get fed."

I am the living bread that came down from heaven. If anyone eats of this bread, he will live forever. This bread is my flesh, which I will give for the life of this world. . . . I tell you the truth, unless you eat the flesh of the Son of Man and drink his blood, you have no life in you. (John 6:51–53)

Upon hearing it, many of His disciples said, "This is a hard teaching. Who can accept it?" But Jesus said to them, "Does this offend you? What if you see the Son of Man ascend to where he was before! The Spirit gives life; the flesh counts for nothing. The words I have spoken to you are spirit and they are life. Yet there are some of you who do not believe" (John 6:60–64).

If this were all Jesus had said on the subject, I have no doubt it would have been the supreme puzzle of His teaching. The bluntness of the way it translates into our language is bound to leave the reader befuddled. But like many of Jesus' discourses, He gave them piecemeal until the final moment. Then the disciples harked back to the first instance when He hinted at the truth. This is clearly the hint. The fulfillment was to follow just days before His death and be finally understood only after His death.

Let us track the event that explained this puzzle.

First of all, it is patently obvious that He could not have meant a literal eating of His physical flesh and His physical blood because He was there in the flesh giving them a piece of bread, not a piece of His flesh.

Second, if He meant His actual flesh and blood, it would be tantamount to saying that only a small number could have shared in that life He offered. It would be restricted to the finite number of pieces a human body could be broken into.

Third, it would be chronologically restrictive. That body would soon decay and the blood would no longer bear life. Only those present at His physical death would have been able to share in that consumption.

Fourth, He had already said that He would raise up that body after it was killed, so that the body itself could not be referred to without making the whole process a masquerade.

Fifth, He commanded the Church to repeat what He was doing across history as a throwback to that moment. That would be impossible with His literal body.

Sixth, He said that His words were Spirit and not flesh.

And finally, when the actual moment of His sacrifice came as He had predicted it would, He explained what it meant. He sat down for the Passover meal with His disciples. The food that sustained, the fellowship this provided, the celebration it encompassed, and the pleasure of God's provision were enjoyed. Only now, there was a heaviness in their hearts. For that heaviness, manna alone would not help. This was a time to face life's supreme worth. An offering of such worth was in the making. The sacrificial Lamb of God was blessing the meal even as He was to be sacrificed. He took the bread, gave thanks, and gave it to His disciples, saying, "Take and eat. This is My body given for you; do this in remembrance of Me." He took the cup, gave thanks, and said, "This cup is the new covenant in My blood, which is poured out for many for the forgiveness of sins." They tasted, touched, smelled, knew, and felt the dimensions of their salvation. He was physically present as He offered the elements.

Then He went on to say, "I tell you, I will not drink of this fruit of the vine from now until that day when I drink it anew with you in My Father's kingdom."

There you have it. This broken piece of bread *represented* what was about to happen. He was going to be physically and emotionally battered in a way that would draw the attention of friend and foe alike. Yet, in that actual brokenness, a mending would ensue. We ourselves would have the way provided to reconnect with God, with our fellow human beings and with ourselves. We would have access to a new relationship, which is part of a larger body, individually and corporately, because of His body broken for us. We could be part of an unbreakable fellowship because He would come and dwell within us. We could take part in an eternal celebration when we would be in the presence of God forever. We could know pleasure at His right hand because worship would be its climactic expression. These symbols of His body broken for ours, His binding for our dismemberment—these are given a tangible expression in the elements when we gather together for worship.

Although by remembering Jesus' past teaching the disciples had a partial understanding of what was happening that night, they were still unclear about all that it meant. That clarity was attained in a significant moment after the resurrection. The day Christ died had been a day they could not understand or appreciate. They saw His body broken, and their lives were devastated. They had questions galore and no one to ask them of.

After Jesus' crucifixion, some of the disciples were returning to their homes, and as they walked on the road toward the town of Emmaus, a stranger came alongside them. Much had happened during those few days, and they were in deep discussion, trying to understand it all. The stranger, listening in, asked why they were so despondent. They told him of the tragic happenings in the death of Jesus three days previous and added, "Are you the only one in Israel who does not know what has happened?"

The truth is that He was the only one in Israel who *did* know what had happened. But they did not yet know who He was. He began to expound all of history and how it tied into that day and its events. They were wonder-struck at the way everything connected. They still did not know who He was and pleaded with Him to stay and have the evening meal with them.

As they sat down to eat, the defining moment came. He broke some bread. And the Bible says that as He did that, their eyes were suddenly opened, and they knew it was Jesus Himself. There has not been a simpler act in history with more profound transhistorical memory attached. What a moment! What a meal! What a message! What a transcendence!

Indeed, to this very day, the Christian sits down with his or her fellow believers and shares in the broken bread and the cup. In that simple trans-action, all of history finds its meaning in the person of Christ. Jesus' death in the past is remembered in the present and points to the future when we will break bread with Him in eternity. Every sense is brought into play—touching, tasting, smelling, hearing, and seeing. In that act, every barrier is broken—the barrier of sin between us and God, the barrier between body and soul as the physical and the spiritual connect, the barrier between life and death, the barrier of race and prejudice—for we all stand before Him at the same meal. It is the "Mensef of God." Can there be a greater reason to celebrate? Now life can be realized with every moment that it is lived.

In his book *Life After God*, Douglas Coupland tells a fascinating story. He was out on a walk in a beautiful park when he came upon a group of blind women, picnicking for the day. When they heard him walking by, they asked him if he would take a picture of them. He gladly consented, and they all snuggled close to get into the picture. But after he left, he pondered, "What on earth would a group of people devoid of sight want a picture for?"[5]

May I suggest that in the way God has fashioned us, He enables us to enjoy the capacity of someone else so that we might share in a benefit even without the ability to experience it. The pictures were probably shown to those with sight, who could add to the insight of these women who, in their memories, could relive the occasion, transcending the way they had lived it the first time.

In this unique moment in history, by offering a broken piece of bread, God brings both sight and insight to the participant through the life of the One whose body was broken and who can therefore lift him or her into a sacred memory. And in that simple act, He refashions him into a new wholeness. That broken bread bridges every humanly unbridgeable chasm in millions of lives. We see in a way nothing else could have imparted—through His eyes, with His presence.

TRANSLATING INTO LIFE

In the practice of the Christian faith, this sharing of the bread and of the cup has been aptly called Communion. God has come near, and we enjoy the indwelling of His presence in us. The contrast here from every other faith is as diametric as one can imagine.

Hinduism at its heart and in its goals teaches us that we are to seek union with the divine. Why union? Because the Hindu claims that we are part and parcel of this divine universe. The goal of the individual is, therefore, to discover that divinity and live it out.

Listen again to the words of Deepak Chopra on this purpose of life. He makes this assertion in the early part of his book: "In reality, we are divinity in disguise, and the gods and goddesses in embryo that are contained within us seek to be fully materialized. True success is therefore the experience of the miraculous. It is the unfolding of the divinity within us."[6]

Later in his book, Chopra makes a statement that forms the basis of his philosophy: "We must find out for ourselves that inside us is a god or goddess in embryo that wants to be born so that we can express our divinity."[7]

I cannot resist asking, Who are the we? Who is the god? Who is the self? Are these different entities with which we are cohabiting? Is there a god who needs me (which me?) to bring him (which him, if it is actually me?) to birth so that my deluded self will cease to be deluded and will emerge divine as the real self? How did this god end up in embryonic form while I became full grown, so that I will give him the privilege of birth and lose my humanity to find my divinity? At the risk of being frivolous, this is the ultimate version of "Who's on first."

Toward the end of his book, Chopra asks us to make a commitment to the beliefs he has espoused in these words:

> Today I will lovingly nurture the god or goddess in embryo that lies deep within my soul. I will pay attention to the spirit within me that animates both my body and my mind. I will awaken myself to this deep stillness within my heart. I will carry the consciousness of timeless, eternal Being in the midst of time-bound experience.[8]

This is the heart of philosophical Hinduism—self-deification. One of India's premier philosophers stated as forthrightly as one could, "Man is God in a temporary state of self-forgetfulness."

How can it be that we are the outworking of the quantum world but at the same time, gods? Is this what a few thousand years of human history have taught us? We are lonely and confused gods who have lost our way? This is the reason the "you" disappears in Hinduism and the meditative process is enjoined, so that we can as individuals merge with the one impersonal absolute—the capital "I," because there is no significant other.[9]

Union with the impersonal absolute defies language, reason, and existential realities. It does not satisfy the longing for communion. However much one may respect the intent of such teaching, we deceive ourselves if we believe that it is philosophically coherent. It is not. That is why some of the most respected Hindu philosophers and thinkers have brandished it as one of the most contradictory systems of life's purpose ever espoused.[10] Not only that, Hinduism could not survive the sterility of this kind of self-deification. Personal deities are erupted by the millions, and the temples are crowded with people seeking to worship. No, the suggestion of inward divinity is psychologically imprisoning and the individual breaks away to find another.

While Hinduism goes to one extreme—the deification of the self—Islam is at the other extreme. In Islam, the distance between God and humanity is so vast that the "I" never gets close to the "Him" in God. And because this distance between the two is impossible to cross, worship takes on an incredible clutter of activity, designed to bring the worshiper close. Repetition and submission take the place of the warmth of a relationship. One need only glimpse a Muslim at worship to see the difference. With all that he observes and all the rules he keeps, there is never a certainty of heaven for the common person in Islam. It is all in the "will of God," they say. One's destiny is left at the mercy of an unknown will. When relationship is swallowed up by rules, political power and enforcement become the means of containment.

One day a Muslim friend and I were out for the day together. I had forgotten that the Fast of Ramadan had just begun and suggested that we step into a restaurant for a cup of coffee. "I will spend years in jail for that cup of coffee," he said, so of course I apologized for the suggestion. Then in low tones he admitted that his fast was restricted to public view and that he did not practice it in private. "I cannot work ten hours a day without eating," he said. There was an awkward silence, and he muttered these words: "I don't think God is the enforcer of these rules." As anyone knows who has asked any Muslim, they will admit with a smile upon their faces that during the month of the Fast of Ramadan more food is sold than during any other month of the year. But its consumption takes place from dusk to dawn rather than from dawn to dusk. Legalism always breeds compliance over purpose.

In the Christian message, the God who is distinct and distant came close so that we who are weak may be made strong and may be drawn close in communion with God Himself, even as our identity is retained as we are. That simple act of communion encapsulated life's purpose. The individual retains his individuality while dwelling in community. The physical retains its physicality but is transcended by the spiritual. The elements retain their distinctness but become bearers of truth that point beyond themselves to a spiritual fellowship that our spirits long for.

Just as the consummate act of love between a man and his wife concretely expresses all that the moral and spiritual relationship embraces, so the simple act of taking the broken bread and the cup encompasses the actual reality of the intermeshing of God's presence in the life of the individual. It is an act of worship that represents a life that is full of meaning. The ramifications are profound.

THE REALITY EXPERIENCED

Let me take you to a unique place at the tip of a desert. I have been there, and my heart has been spoken to in ways beyond description. Walk into a Sunday morning worship service, and this is what you will see. There sit two women missionaries, surrounded by a group of people who, when they smile, look pitiful. When they come closer, you feel a lump in your throat. But they are wonderful people who love Christ. This is a home for people with leprosy. There in that room, the moment of Communion has come. The elements are passed, and the object lesson is staggering.

Beyond the heinousness of the disease emerges a glorious message of oneness and hope. His body is broken for all of us so that His nourishment, His friendship, His celebration, and His pleasure bind us together as one. One day those bodies will all be made new when we drink from that cup and eat from that bread with our heavenly Father.

This brings us to a most staggering conclusion on what *worship* means. Food and health may be a relevant branch to which we hold. But the trunk that is rooted in the sacred call of God to worship is based on a reversal of that relevance. It is not that God needs to be relevant to us. It is the very counterperspective of God that beckons *us* to become relevant to *Him*. What do I mean?

In his book *The Integrity of Worship,* Paul Waitman Hoon includes a chapter called "The Irrelevance of Worship." His whole point is summarized in one paragraph in which he reminds us that the experience of worship can sometimes call us to look beyond our need to what God is calling us toward:

How often have we craved light on our life in the world, only to be summoned to ponder our destiny in eternity. How often have we been preoccupied with the church local, and instead found our vision turned to the Church triumphant and universal. And how often have we asked that worship bless our souls with peace, only to hear the lesson for the day calling us to a holy warfare. How often have we desired strength to overcome the world, only to learn that we are to be stoned and sawn asunder in the world. How often have we sought comfort to our sorrows, and instead found the sorrows of the world added to our own. Such reversals may be strange to men. But only such contradiction answers to realities both relevant and irrelevant that are at the heart of the Church's worship.[11]

This was the reversal the disciples did not expect. They came to Jesus asking for the abundance of bread so their stomachs could be full. They discovered that there was bread of a different kind broken for them because of a deeper emptiness than they had imagined. They had bought their lunch at a nearby restaurant. But they were being invited to a different table. With their purchase, they would soon be hungry again. Jesus was offering them eternal fulfillment with moment-by-moment freshness. That is why the task of the Church is not so much to make God relevant to the people as much as it is to make people relevant to God.

There is a magnificent woodcarving in Worms, Germany, called "The Altar of Blood." It is a depiction of the Lord breaking the bread for the disciples. I stared at that masterpiece, which took years of a craftsman's life to complete, and found it beyond my capability to describe. It is the heart of what God calls us to. It is in that exchange that He sobers the mind, quiets the heart, and bridges every barrier.

Is our God so small that He cannot impart life without cannibalizing? Those who understand the depth of what Communion means understand the fulfillment of worship. Those who don't understand leave hungry and cannibalize their own souls. The songwriter rightly pleads for all of us, so that our deepest hunger may be sated.

> Break Thou the Bread of Life,
> Dear Lord to me,
> As thou didst break the loaves

Beside the sea;
Beyond the sacred page
I seek thee, Lord;
My spirit pants for thee,
O living Word.

Thou art the bread of life,
To me, to me,
Thy holy Word, the truth
That saveth me;
Give me to eat and live
With thee above,
Teach me to love Thy truth
For Thou art love.

Oh, send Thy Spirit, Lord,
Now unto me,
That He may touch my eyes
And make me see;
Show me the truth concealed
Within thy Word,
And in Thy Book revealed,
I see Thee Lord.[12]

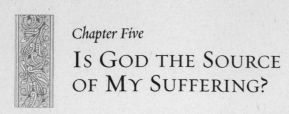

Chapter Five

Is God the Source of My Suffering?

I would like to begin this chapter by respectfully quoting, with the permission of the writer, portions of one of the most heartbreaking letters I have ever received. I truly admire the courage, the candor, and the teachability of the man who wrote it. It is obviously not easy to bare one's soul. My heart aches for him and his family in this terribly painful experience.

This letter, though specific and immediate in the writer's context, represents a question asked of Jesus two thousand years ago, in a similar situation. In fact, for all of us, if we are honest, behind this question lies possibly one of the greatest barriers to belief in God.

Dear Mr. Zacharias,

I need your help desperately. I'm not asking for money or anything like that. . . . I seek your counsel.

Please take time to read this letter. It is extremely personal and heartbreaking. My situation is serious, and I am now well into my second year of torment and fear. I thought I would be able to figure out all the "answers" I would need to find peace in my soul but have continually run into the proverbial brick wall. Or perhaps the answer was there all the time and it is just too grim for me to accept. I don't know. Quite simply I am confused and frightened. And I need your help.

On August 4, 1997, at 3:15 P.M., my son, Adam Mark Triplett, died in an airplane accident. It happened in the town of New Richmond, Wisconsin. Adam was a flight instructor for a local flight school in St. Paul, Minnesota. Adam was a respected student, fine musician, professional pilot, devoted friend, and dedicated Christian man. He was also a delightful brother, husband, and son. My only son. Adam died at the age of 23, after only three months of marriage. I can't imagine life without him. . . .

A few years ago my wife and I purchased a new computer. Little did I know how much danger it would bring into my life. One day, casually exploring the Internet with my newfound friend of technology, I was surprised to discover an e-mail message sent to me anonymously. To my shock and surprise, I found myself looking at a picture of perversion and hard-core pornography.

I became angered by this vulgar intrusion and set out to find out more of where it came from. I continued my search, thinking I could become a crusader of sorts for the cause of decency. But I fell victim to the wiles and devices of the devil himself and soon became trapped in a pattern of personal viewing.

If I had a "bad day" at work or the car broke down (any excuse would do), I would settle the score as it were by balancing the scales with a bit of "personal viewing." By now I justified my "personal viewing" as not harmful. . . . I wasn't intruding on or hurting anyone else. I paid no attention to what I was doing to myself.

One day at church I found myself in "personal viewing" in my mind, not paying attention to the pastor's message. Fear jumped into my heart, and I began to try to do away with this evil practice. No success. The downward spiral continued, affecting my business and family relationships, to say nothing of my responsibilities as a leader in my church.

On August 4, I dropped my son off at the airport. His next student was waiting for him. As he walked away from the car he turned and smiled and gave me a "thumbs-up" sign (our personal sign of approval). As I drove away, looking in the rearview mirror . . . I had a strange and faint realization that it would be the last time I would ever see him on earth. I shook it off as a random thought. I discarded it. Forgot it completely. I went back to work.

By the end of the day I was in a steep rage over God only knows what . . . [and I decided that] I would just go home and do some "personal viewing." At least I could find some satisfaction there, I thought.

[As I was driving,] very quietly, almost in a whisperlike tone, soft and gentle, in a pleading voice I felt God saying to me, "Mark, please, I don't want you to do that."

My response was harsh and direct, "Oh, You don't want me to. Big deal! You don't want me to do anything, do You? I always have to be perfect, don't I? Well, not today!" The Lord then spoke a bit louder and more serious, "I'm asking you not to behave this way." Again I responded with arrogance, "How are You going to stop me? What will You do, kill my son?"

A third time the Lord God spoke to me. But this time His tone was more forceful, strict, and authoritative, "Mark, you don't understand. I'm telling you that I do NOT want you behaving this way."

By now, my ego was in full swing. My response was deliberate and direct. I heard no more from the Lord regarding the issue.

I arrived home at about 5:30. My wife was cooking on the grill in the backyard. She asked me if I had heard of a plane crash that day. I said no. She seemed unnerved and suspicious and afraid. I "felt" something was wrong. . . .

Then the sheriff arrived. Katrina (Adam's sister) screamed. Linda wept uncontrollably. I was completely numb but felt a presence of strength take over my body and mind. I believe it was God's Holy Spirit. . . .

In the weeks that followed Adam's death, I began recalling the events of that day. I became consumed with the guilt of my sin against God that day. I became acutely aware of my wretchedness and the need to fall at His feet and seek forgiveness. . . . Was I to blame for this horror? Oh, dear God, let it not be so.[1]

As you can well imagine, this letter stopped my day. As I read it, with each paragraph the anguish intensified, as blood flooding into emptied arteries. My heart throbbed, beating out sensations of self-examination. Everything else faded into secondary importance. I put myself in this man's shoes and imagined the horror.

How much more painful can life be than to carry such enormous guilt, laden on top of such tragedy? When the wording was narrowed down, the sharp question remained, "Did God take my son's life? Was He making me pay for going against His wishes?"

This double-pronged search for an answer—"Is God the author of pain?" "Is my pain because of my sin?"—has disturbed both skeptic and believer alike. Every thinking person attempting to make sense of a world enriched with good but convulsing with evil tries to think this through, yet finds no easy solution, especially when something as dramatic as this happens. After centuries of debate, to find an adequate response remains a daunting task. It is a question worthy of our greatest attention. At the same time, I am convinced that there is no more comprehensive answer to the problem of suffering and evil than the one that the Christian faith affords.

The Bible does not avoid raising this struggle. Jesus faced this question head-on. Sometimes it came to Him in subtle forms, sometimes in direct tones. The most striking incident in which He faced this challenge is recorded in the ninth chapter of John's Gospel. The discussion ensues on the heels of one of the lengthiest reports of any miracle that He performed. There is more than normal dialogue that precedes and succeeds this particular healing, and the reason is because an explanation is sought for a person's physical deformity.

As Jesus was walking along with His disciples, a man who was blind crossed their path. The disciples, in this instance, were not content just to witness the miracle of sight restored. They went for the jugular, aiming quite clearly at the role of God in a tragic situation. One of the disciples asked Jesus rather abruptly, "Who sinned, this man or his parents, that he was born blind?"

Is he responsible for his plight, or is someone else the cause?

Jesus completely surprised them with His response that it was neither the young man nor his parents who were responsible for the man's deformity. "This happened so that the work of God might be displayed in his life. As long as it is day, we must do the work of Him who sent Me. Night is coming when no man can work. While I am in the world, I am the Light of the World."

What did He mean, "That the work of God might be displayed in his life"?

As He tried to unfold the answer, bear in mind that He was up against four groups of people, each with their own reason for questioning Him. The first were the disciples themselves. They wanted this question answered because they sought an explanation of individual suffering. But then there were the neighbors. They knew a miracle had taken place and were puzzled at the "how" of it all. How could He give sight to the blind? The skeptics in the group literally saw the effect but did not want to admit the "Who" behind it. They did not like where Jesus' answer led them because it compelled them to decide whether or not they had the honesty to repudiate their pride and follow Him. And finally, there was the blind man himself. He had personally experienced the transformation and was somewhat overwhelmed by all of the implications—especially, facing the critics. A personal conversation with Jesus left him without doubt that He was not merely a healer of the eyes; He was the transformer of the heart.

It is obvious that Jesus' answer in this passage goes beyond the agonies of parents who have lost children or of those who have graciously borne much pain. He recognized immediately that there was a question behind the question.

The answer, therefore, goes deeper, not only to touch the pain of the human heart but to understand the breadth of evil, pain, and suffering. If we are to go as deep, the answer necessarily will take us through a long journey. The question simply cannot be answered while ignoring possible challenges to the answer at every stage. Those who stay with it will see that the biblical world-view is the only one that accepts the reality of evil and suffering while giving both the cause and the purpose, while offering God-given strength and sustenance in the midst of it. Those who refuse to accept these truths that Jesus presents will continue to find this a barrier to God and, I dare suggest, a barrier to reason itself.

Years ago, there was a lighthearted story making the rounds. It was the story of a breakdown in a power plant that sent the city into confusion. For a long time, no engineer could be found who was able to fix the problem. Finally a man came along who, by the push of a button, restarted the system. He billed the city for a million and one dollars. Surprised at the number, somebody asked him why it was a million and one, and not just a million. His answer was that one dollar was for pushing the button. The one million dollars was for knowing where to push.

At first glance, Jesus' response to their question seems rather meager. It consists of a few simple statements. But those brief lines are weighted with comprehension on a larger scale. That is why the incredible depth in Jesus' answer can only be appreciated if the world-view behind it is understood. To just take hold of these few lines and miss the context of His total message is to do violence to a very important theme. To avoid that peril, I will take the question back to its underlying challenge and face the hard but real struggle of evil and pain in a world to which a loving God lays claim. Once we have comprehended the broader Christian perspective, we will understand that Christ readily answers the immediate question in light of the bigger question behind it.

A UNIVERSAL ANGUISH

At the outset, let us remember that *every* world-view—not just Christianity's—must give an explanation or an answer for evil and suffering. Either evil categorically proves that God does not exist, as the atheist avows, or evil is "not ultimately real evil," as the pantheist claims, or evil is most coherently explained by the Christian view of God and His purpose in creation. In short, this is not a problem distinctive to Christianity. It will not do for the challenger just to raise the question. This problem of evil is one to which we all must offer an answer, regardless of the belief system to which we subscribe.

Among the discoveries I have made as I have studied this subject is that every writer who attempts to answer this question has one thing in common with all others and one fundamental assumption. The common factor is that each one begins with a litany of horrors and atrocities. It is not just one person born blind, or one baby innocently killed. The list seems interminable. It is as if we ourselves need reminders of how emotionally charged this problem is, defying any reasonable solution. Horrors of unimaginable proportions are cataloged. I found that in itself instructive, and this approach has a lesson that I will address later.

But then there emerges a second component, and that is the determination of a starting point. Much is assumed or concealed right at the beginning. For the skeptic, the question ties him or her up, immediately. That confusion ought to pay heed to the Irish farmer who, when asked for directions by a lost tourist, said, "If that is where you want to go, this is not where I would begin." You see, most skeptics begin their challenge to God's existence with the problem of evil or at least reserve their greatest emotion for that discussion. But in doing so, they dig a deeper pit than the one they are trying to get out of, because raising the problem of evil without God runs the risk of failing to justify the question. But many do begin here and get wrongheaded. As this discussion proceeds, I will point out why this is not a logically sound starting point for one who seeks to disprove the existence of God.

POSITIONING THE PROBLEM

The Christian world-view suggests that evil is better posed as a mystery than as a problem. Now, before the antagonist jumps up and cries, "Foul!" thinking that by branding it a mystery I am attempting to evade a solution, let me calm that fear. To call it a mystery is not to avoid the necessity of realizing a solution. Problems seek answers, but mysteries demand more—they merit explanation. This means that there will need to be converging lines of argument, not just a single answer signed off with Q.E.D.

But there is a very important reason to brand evil a mystery. Gabriel Marcel defined a mystery as a problem that encroaches on its own data. By that he meant that the questioner unwittingly becomes the object of the question. We are not merely observers to the reality of evil. We are involved in it beyond any mere academic discussion. Peter Kreeft, professor of philosophy at Boston College, comments, "Getting to Mars is a problem. Falling in love is a mystery."[2] Evil, like love, is not a problem. It is a mystery.

One cannot address the problem of evil without ending up as a focus of that problem. Skeptics calmly bypass this reality and proceed as if they were spectators observing a phenomenon, when in reality, they are part of the phenomenon. Let us position the challenge to Christian theism in the words of the renowned thinker David Hume, and we will quickly see how the question carries the questioner with it. This is how he words it:

> Were a stranger to drop on a sudden into this world, I would show him, as a specimen of its ills, a hospital full of diseases, a prison crowded with malefactors and debtors, a field of battle strewn with carcasses, a fleet floundering in the ocean, a nation languishing under tyranny, famine, or pestilence. To turn the gay side of

life to him, and give him a notion of its pleasures; whither should I conduct him? to a ball, to an opera, to court? He might justly think that I was only showing him a diversity of distress and sorrow.[3]

Hume complains elsewhere that it is impossible to square such a world with an ultimate purpose of love. This is possibly better posed than Hume even realized, for he hinted at an explanation even in the question. The thrust of his question is forthright. The problem of pain and suffering is real and individually felt. That is why every group got involved with Jesus on this matter.

Not only is the problem real and felt, it is also universal. No religion attempts to explain this more than Buddhism. Buddha's entire pilgrimage toward "Enlightenment" began because of his absorption with the mystery of evil and suffering. The universality of it was what set him on his course.

But if there is the reality of it and the universality of it, there is also the complexity of it. Evil is questioned from at least three sides: the metaphysical problem (What is the source of it?), the physical problem (How do natural disasters, etc., fit into the discussion?), and the moral problem (How can it be justified?).

The third of these is at the heart of the issue: How does a good God allow so much suffering? Immediately we enter into a very serious dilemma. How do you respond to the intellectual side of the question without losing the existential side of it? How do you answer the Mark Tripletts of this world without drowning it all in philosophy?

Those who feel the pain of the question most, often shudder at how theoretical philosophical answers are. We do not like to work through the intellectual side of the question because we do not see where logic and philosophy fit into the problem of pain. If you have just buried a son or a daughter, or have witnessed brutality firsthand, this portion of the argument may bring more anger than comfort. Who wants logic when the heart is broken? Who wants a physiological treatise on the calcium component of the bone when the shoulder has come out of its socket? At such a time we are looking for comfort. We want a painkiller.

But to focus only on the result without paying due heed to the process may only temporarily kill the pain, leaving the joint still out of order.

Somewhere and at some point, logic must stand on its own. Comfort will follow if the reasoning is surefooted.

And to you, the reader, I plead: Even if this first portion seems tedious, please stay with it, because it is here that we study the question, before proceeding to the answer. We must not allow the anguish of the heart to bypass the reasoning of the mind. The explanation must meet both the intellectual and the emotional demands of the question. Answering the questions of the mind while ignoring shredded emotions seems heartless. Binding the emotional wounds while ignoring the struggle of the intellect seems mindless.

What, then, is the starting point? Since the crux of the problem is first and foremost moral questioning, how can there be moral justification for evil? An analogy from C. S. Lewis may be of help. He reminded us that when a ship is on the high seas, at least three questions must be answered. Question number one, How do we keep the ship from sinking? Number two, How do we keep it from bumping into other ships? These two may be obvious but behind them lurks the most important one, number three, Why is the ship out there in the first place? The first of the questions deals with personal ethics. The second addresses social ethics. The third one wrestles with normative ethics.

Our cultures at best deal with the first and the second questions. They ignore a rational defense of the very purpose of life and do not know where to turn for guidance. If one does not know one's purpose, any destination will do. And when the ship starts to sink or bumps into another ship, how does one safely reach the harbor without any instruments?

Let us be certain that no ethical imperative can be established and no moral pronouncements can be made without first establishing life's imperative and knowing how to measure progress. Why do we exist, anyway? And it is here that the skeptic flounders on the high seas of life. If we are here purely by accident and we navigate purely by whim, how does one determine whether any journey is in the right or wrong direction? Why be in one place rather than anywhere else?

Now we shall see why the question itself defeats the skeptic who at the same time wants to deny that any purpose for life actually exists.

LIVING WITH CONTRADICTION

Let me present two doors through which the person who has raised the question of God's existence tries to escape from the entailments of disbelief with the semblance of a reason. I am afraid, however, that those doors are marked "No Exit."

The first escape route in the problem of evil is propounded by those who protest that God cannot exist because there is too much evil evident in life. They see no logical contradiction within their system since they do not have to prove that evil coexists with a good Creator. Evil exists; therefore, the Creator does not. That is categorically stated.

But here, Christianity provides a counterchallenge to remind them that they have not escaped the problem of contradiction. If evil exists, then one must assume that good exists in order to know the difference. If good exists, one must assume that a moral law exists by which to measure good and evil. But if a moral law exists, must not one posit an ultimate source of moral law, or at least an objective basis for a moral law? By an objective basis, I mean something that is transcendingly true at all times, regardless of whether I believe it or not.

This argument is very compelling and must be given due consideration by anyone who denies the existence of God but accepts the presence of evil. In contrast to the Christian's assertion that God is necessary in order to posit the notions of good and evil, the skeptic responds by asking, "Why cannot evolution explain our moral sense? Why do we need God?"

This is the latest approach by antitheistic thinkers who seek to explain good and evil apart from God. Over the years naturalists first denied causality as an argument to prove God's existence: Why do we have to have a cause? Why can't the universe just be? Then they denied design as an argument for God's existence: Why do we need a designer? Why could it not have all just come together with the appearance of design? Now they deny morality as an argument for God's existence: Why do we need to posit a moral law or a moral law source? Why can't it just be a pragmatic reality? This I find fascinating! They want a *cause* for suffering or a *design* for suffering, but they have already denied that either of these is necessary to account for every effect.

This attempt to deny God because of the presence of evil is so fraught with the illogical that one marvels at its acceptance. Not one proponent of evolutionary ethics has explained how an impersonal, amoral first cause through a nonmoral process has produced a moral basis of life, while at the same time denying any objective moral basis for good and evil. Does it not seem odd that of all the permutations and combinations that a random universe might afford we should end up with the notions of the true, the good, and the beautiful? In reality, why call anything good or evil? Why not call it orange or purple? That way, we settle it as different preferences. By the way, Bertrand Russell tried that latter approach and looked quite pathetic at it.

The truth is that we cannot escape the existential rub by running from a moral law. Objective moral values exist only if God exists. Is it all right, for example, to mutilate babies for entertainment? Every reasonable person will say no. We know that objective moral values do exist. Therefore God must exist. Examining those premises and their validity presents a very strong argument. In fact, J. L. Mackie, one of the most vociferous atheists who challenged the existence of God on the basis of the reality of evil, granted at least this logical connection when he said:

> We might well argue . . . that objective intrinsically prescriptive features, supervenient upon natural ones, constitute so odd a cluster of qualities and relations that they are most unlikely to have arisen in the ordinary course of events, without an all-powerful God to create them.[4]

Therefore, the conclusion must be agreed upon that nothing can be intrinsically, prescriptively good unless there also exists a God who has fashioned the universe thus. But that is the very Being skeptics want to deny because of the existence of evil.

The first exit door to flee from God is opened, and the sight is terrifying. Only one option is left, and that is to try to alter the shape of the door. Recognizing that if evil is admitted then an objective moral law might need to be invoked, the skeptic tries a new tack. Listen to this incredible explanation by one of atheism's champions, Richard Dawkins, of Oxford:

In a universe of blind physical forces and genetic replication, some people are going to get hurt, other people are going to get lucky, and you won't find any rhyme or reason in it, nor any justice. The universe we observe has precisely the properties we should expect if there is, at the bottom, no design, no purpose, no evil and no other good. Nothing but blind, pitiless indifference. DNA neither knows nor cares. DNA just is. And we dance to its music.[5]

Do you see what has happened? The skeptic started by presenting a long list of horrific things, saying, "These are immoral, therefore there is no God." But to raise these issues as moral issues is to assume a state of affairs that evolution cannot afford. There is just no way to arrive at a morally compelling ought, given the assumptions of naturalism. What then does the skeptic do? He denies objective moral values because to accept such a reality would be to allow for the possibility of God's existence. He concludes then that there really isn't such a thing as evil after all.

This is supposed to be an answer? If DNA neither knows nor cares, what is it that prompts *our* knowing and *our* caring? Are we just embodied computers, overvaluing our senses? If our feelings have no bearing at all on the reality of this question then maybe *ours* is the artificial intelligence and the computer's is the genuine one, for it has no feeling; it has only information. Computers do not "care" and do not "grieve over evil," and are, therefore, closer to reality.

Is this what we have come to? We must be warned that there are no brakes on this slippery slope once we step onto it. The denial of an objective moral law, based on the compulsion to deny the existence of God, results ultimately in the denial of evil itself. Can you imagine telling a raped woman that the rapist merely danced to his DNA? Tell the father of young Adam Triplett that he is merely dancing to his DNA. Tell the victims of Auschwitz that their tormentors merely danced to their DNA, and tell the loved ones of those cannibalized by Jeffrey Dahmer that he merely danced to his DNA. So dance along!

How repugnant! This is not a dance! This is the escapist's foot on the throat of reason, gasping for rationality while denying that logical points of reference exist. In effect, while seeking an answer to the question of evil, he ends up denying the question. In fact, I put this theory to the test with some students at Oxford University. I asked a group of skeptics if I took a baby and sliced it to pieces before them, would I have done anything wrong? They had just denied that objective moral values exist. At my question, there was silence, and then the lead voice in the group said, "I would not like it, but no, I could not say you have done anything wrong." My! What an aesthete. He would not like it. My! What irrationality—he could not brand it wrong. I only had to ask him what then remains of the original question, if evil is denied?

Dawkins could have helped him even further. In his 1992 lectures to the British Humanist Association, he made an astounding assertion. Having debunked the notion of God in his numerous writings and explained away evil as DNA's dance, what then must we make of the sense of morality that we find in the human experience? Why do we even pose such questions about good and evil?

Dawkins has the answer. Viruses. A virus scrambles the data within the human gene and spits out this misinformation. Somehow if we can expunge the virus that led us to think this way, we will be purified and rid of this bedeviling notion of God, good, and evil.[6]

In Dawkins-speak, those who asked Jesus the question needed an antivirus program. In fact, Jesus Himself would need reprogramming. And I suppose, one who moralizes on the Holocaust needs new antivirus protection. That way the question of evil would not even surface. One would like to ask Dawkins if we are morally bound to remove that virus. Let us not forget that he himself is, of course, free from the virus and can therefore input our moral data.

The problem has encroached upon itself. In an attempt to escape what they call the contradiction between a good God and a world of evil, skeptics exorcise the mind of theistic notions, only to be entered and overcome by contradictions sevenfold.

Though I have often quoted G. K. Chesterton in his criticism of this kind of thinking, no one says it better, so I would like to quote him again:

All denunciation implies a moral doctrine of some kind and the modern skeptic doubts not only the institution he denounces, but the doctrine by which he denounces it. Thus he writes one book complaining that imperial oppression insults the purity of women, and then writes another book, a novel in which he insults it himself. As a politician he will cry out that war is a waste of life, and then as a philosopher that all of life is waste of time. A Russian pessimist will denounce a policeman for killing a peasant, and then prove by the highest philosophical principles that the peasant ought to have killed himself. A man denounces marriage as a lie and then denounces aristocratic profligates for treating it as a lie.

The man of this school goes first to a political meeting where he complains that savages are treated as if they were beasts. Then he takes his hat and umbrella and goes on to a scientific meeting where he proves that they practically are beasts. In short, the modern revolutionist, being an infinite skeptic, is forever engaged in undermining his own mines. in his book on politics he attacks men for trampling on morality; in his book on ethics he attacks morality for trampling on men. Therefore the modern man in revolt becomes practically useless for all purposes of revolt. By rebelling against everything he has lost his right to rebel against anything.[7]

Let me illustrate Chesterton's point with something more contemporary. In pathetic ways, we saw this exemplified when America was caught in the throes of the Clinton-Lewinsky scandal. In our moral contradiction, an amazing cultural mood was uncovered. The president's famous line that "it all depends on what the definition of 'is' is," sent reporters scampering onto the streets with the question of the century: "Do words have a fixed meaning, or may we give them any meaning we choose?" (What could encroach upon itself more than purveyors of words inquiring if words have any meaning, while using words to ask the question?)

To the utter "surprise" of the surveyors, most people seemed to agree that words can sometimes mean different things to different people, assuming, of course, that there was no equivocation in meaning as the question was posed and the answer given.

That prompted the next question: "Is morality an absolute or a private matter?" The overwhelming response came back that morality is a private matter.

These two questions became the lead-in on a CNN news report. First, that words only have personal meaning. Second, that morality is a private matter. Ironically, the third item on the news was that the United States had just issued a stern warning to Saddam Hussein that if he did not stop playing word games with the nuclear inspection teams we would start bombing Iraq. Suddenly, words did matter. We would not let Saddam dance to *his* DNA. We would not let him write *his* own dictionary. We would not let him live by *his* own ethic, but we could let each of *our* citizens determine the meaning of the words they used and insist that our morality is no one else's business.

This is precisely the world to which Dawkins and those of similar philosophy must be logically driven. It is a world of systemic contradiction. If morality is nothing more than evolution's climb, there is no way to measure when we have reached the top. By their own admission, there was no prevision in the random collocation of atoms. In the end, such a philosophy of evil makes life unlivable in a community. Dawkins cannot explain evil by denying an objective moral law, and he cannot deny evil without losing his challenge for the existence of God. This door for the skeptic is marked "No Exit," even as his ship sinks.

ASKING GOD TO BE CONTRADICTORY

The second door seems, at first, to be a certain way out. The skeptic asks why God could not have made us to always choose good. Philosophers of note have raised this as the sharpest edge of their challenge to Christianity. But here, too, the challenge violates reason.

Alvin Plantinga of the University of Notre Dame, who is considered by many to be the most respected Protestant philosopher of our time, has made a strong and compelling argument against this challenge of the skeptic. He argues that this option bears a false view of what God's omnipotence means. We must realize that God cannot do that which is mutually exclusive and logically impossible. God cannot make square circles. The terms are mutually exclusive.

Plantinga is right. I might add that if God *can* do anything at all, even that which is mutually exclusive, then He can also contradict His character, which would by implication render the problem of evil moot, needing no defense. The very reason we raise the question is because we seek coherence. In a world where love is the supreme ethic, freedom must be built in. A love that is programmed or compelled is not love; it is merely a conditioned response or self-serving.

Once again, even thinkers hostile to Christianity inadvertently assert truths that agree with Christian thought. For example, Jean Paul Sartre, in *Being and Nothingness,* says:

> The man who wants to be loved does not desire the enslavement of the beloved. He is not bent on becoming the object of passion, which flows forth mechanically. He does not want to possess an automaton, and if we want to humiliate him, we need try to only persuade him that the beloved's passion is the result of a psychological determinism. The lover will then feel that both his love and his being are cheapened. . . . If the beloved is transformed into an automaton, the lover finds himself alone.[8]

How insightful! Love compelled is a precursor to loneliness. Having the freedom to love when you may choose not to love is to give love legitimate meaning. This is why I said earlier that David Hume had more of an answer in his question on the problem of pain than he may have known. Is not an ultimate purpose of love the only way you *can* square the problem of pain? To ask that we be denied freedom and only choose good is to ask not for love, but for compulsion and for something other than humanity.

Both doors of escape for the skeptic are shut tight. You cannot posit evil without a transcendent moral law, which macroevolution cannot sustain. And you cannot gain the highest ethic without the possibility of freedom. The first sends us into lives of contradiction. The second demands a contradiction of God.

In brief, for the naturalist, the man born blind was dancing to his DNA. As to the question behind the question, the naturalist not only fails to answer it, he fails even to justify it.

How would other religions answer the disciples' question, and the question behind the question?

As I have stated, pantheistic religions have attempted extensive answers, and sometimes those answers are terribly confusing. The difficulty with Hinduism is that it has no monolithic answer to the problem of suffering. By declaring everything in the physical world to be nonreal, illusory, changing, transitory, it ends up with philosophical problems beyond measure. And, of course, one is compelled to ask, What has brought on this "illusion" of evil, if everything is part and parcel of the divine reality? They do try to answer that.

There is a classic passage in the Bhagavad-Gita in which Krishna counsels young Arjuna, who is on the battlefield, facing the possibility of killing his own half brothers. He struggles and cannot bring himself to do this. Krishna, who comes as his chariot-driver, talks to him about his duty. This was his duty, to fulfill his caste's responsibility as a warrior. This is the way life moves on. But he told Arjuna not to fear to do his duty, for all good and evil are fused in the one ultimate reality, Brahman. In Brahman, says Krishna, the distinction breaks down. That which appears evil is only the lesser reality. In the end, all life, all good, all evil, flow from God and back to Him or it. "Go to war and do your job." This convergence of everything into one absolute reality forms the hub of the answer to the question behind the question. One can see how a sense of fatalism dominates when all reality is inexorably and inevitably unfolding.

There is a humorous story told of India's leading philosopher, Shankara. He had just finished lecturing the king on the deception of the mind and its delusion of material reality. The next day, the king let loose an elephant that went on a rampage, and Shankara ran up a tree to find safety. When the king asked him why he ran if the elephant was nonreal, Shankara, not to be outdone, said, "What the king actually saw was a nonreal me climbing up a nonreal tree!" One might add, "That is a nonreal answer."

While these are seen as fables, there is no way for classical Hinduism to deal with the problem of evil. To deny that evil is real does not diminish wickedness, nor does it daunt the heart's desire to seek purity. So much of

Hindu worship is steeped in purification rites. That is why the entire corpus of popular Hinduism is filled with the forms of worship, fear of punishment, means of obtaining God's favor, etc.

But why are these hungers themselves seen as real? In fact, one of Hinduism's strongest criticisms of Christianity and the reason given for refusing its validity is the Hindu's reference to the days of the British Raj and to the evil of the exploitation of the subjugated. One cannot have it both ways; evil cannot be both illusory and concrete.

Hinduism explains this perception of evil as induced by ignorance. But that only pushes the question one step further. If all is one, and plurality is an illusion born out of ignorance, then who is the source of the ignorance but the one? And if the one is the source of the ignorance, then the impersonal absolute in the one is an absolute that lacks true knowledge. But here we face Hinduism's real answer to the question of the man who was blind from birth.

Reincarnation is a central feature of Hindu philosophy. In fact, some eastern thinkers have leaped upon this particular passage of the blind man as proof that the Bible teaches reincarnation. How else could the man have sinned before birth? Let us be assured that it is both a misrepresentation of the passage and an avoidance of facing up to what their doctrine of reincarnation actually espouses.

First, this section hardly "teaches" reincarnation. It is merely a question asked. The Bible's teaching is that "it is appointed unto men *once* to die, but after this the judgment" (Heb. 9:27 KJV; emphasis added). In fact, in this very context Jesus states that there was no direct connection between any previous act and the man's condition, and that the opportunity to choose to believe God's message is brief, after which there is no recourse. By contrast and by definition, reincarnation is a recurring cycle of cause and effect, till all infractions have been paid for and the absolute attained. Jesus clearly denies that possibility. "Night is coming when no man can work," He said. Opportunity ends.

Rather than hearing my thoughts on what reincarnation in Hinduism means, listen instead, to the words of the Upanishads on this matter:

Accordingly, those who are of pleasant conduct here—the prospect is, indeed, that they will enter a pleasant womb, either the womb of a Brahman [the priestly class], or the womb of a Kshatriya [the warrior or royal class], or the womb of a Vaisya [the working or professional class]. But those who are of stinking conduct here—the prospect is, indeed, that they will enter a stinking womb of a dog, or the womb of a swine, or the womb of an outcast. (Chandogya Upanishad, 5.10.8)

There are other passages of descriptions that go into further detail, ideas that one cannot read with indifference. Hinduism here conveys an inherited sense of wrong, which is lived out in the next life, in vegetable, animal, or human form. This doctrine is nonnegotiable in Hindu philosophy. There are passages in the Upanishads that are rather jolting, when one reads them.

Buddhism also invokes the doctrine of karma and reincarnation. The opening lines of the Buddhist scriptures say that every individual is the sum total of what he or she thought in his or her past life. One of the collections of Buddha's discourses is called the Anguttara Nikaya. Here are some thoughts:

My *kamma* [past and present actions] is my only property, *kamma* is my only heritage, *kamma* is the only cause of my being, *kamma* is my only kin, my only protection. Whatever actions I do, good or bad, I shall become their heir.[9]

(Take note that the Pali language of the Buddhist scriptures has a different sound to some words that have become common in English from Hinduism. *Kamma*, for example, carries the meaning of *karma*.)

So, for Buddhism, too, the answer to the disciples' question regarding the blind man's predicament—"Who sinned, this man or his parents?"—would be, "Both this man and his parents have sinned." The suffering of the blind man is the inheritance of his past life's sin, and it is the lot of the parents to inherit this situation.

They do have a difference, though. Hinduism argued by saying that behind the world of the transitory or nonreal lies what is ultimately real. Buddhism reversed that by saying that behind the real world is actually impermanence. Thus, the reason for all our cravings is that because we think there is permanence, we have cravings. Once we know there is nothing permanent, not even the self, then we stop craving. In the state of "Enlightenment," the self is extinguished and all desire, and therefore, suffering, is gone. That is the goal of Buddhism.

How can we end suffering? According to Buddhist teaching, if we can obliterate desire we will obliterate evil. In fact, the very word *nirvana* means the negation of the jungle of desire to which our rebirths have condemned us.

Can one resist asking, How does a world-view that considers everything to be impermanent even explain the origin of impermanence and the seduction of the mind to see these as permanent? What, then, is this self if it doesn't even exist, except as an illusion? The answer of Buddha is that he himself lived under the illusion of permanence until through multiple reincarnations he discovered the impermanence of all reality. Then he announced that this would be his last existence, since he had obtained complete desirelessness. In that last incarnation, of course, he corrected his disciples in their erroneous views. He challenged several Hindu teachings.

But above all, Buddhism faces a truly insurmountable problem. If life is cyclical and there is no beginning to the incarnations, why is there an end? How does one have an infinite regress of causes, if there is a final incarnation?

Philosopher William Lane Craig reminds us that an infinite regress of causes is like trying to jump out of a bottomless pit. How do you start if you never reach the bottom? On the other hand, one might well ask, if every birth is a rebirth, what *kamma* was paid for in his first birth? One might also ask that if desirelessness is the ultimate *nirvana,* would it then be safe to say that in that state there is not even the desire to see evil come to an end?

The incredible aspect of this teaching is that the more painful one's existence, the more certain that the previous life is successfully paying its dues. So that when one picks up the body of a little child, deformed from birth, *kamma* is in operation. One might not wish to admit this, but that is the existential reality of this teaching.

Some years ago, I was told of a group of missionaries and their families who had been killed in a bus accident near a village in a Buddhist country. Within minutes, the bus was ransacked and the bodies pillaged for loot. The reason—those who died were only receiving their *kamma,* and there is nothing wrong in taking what is left from one who is paying his or her dues.

If every life is a payment for a previous life, one also wonders why Buddha was so reluctant to allow women into the sacred order and decreed that the rules for governing them be far greater. In fact, even a woman who had been in the order for years owed greater reverence to a man who was just an initiate. If *kamma* is in operation, why were these rules superimposed, assuming a virtue of higher order placed upon some? Unless of course, a woman, by virtue of being a woman, inherited a greater *kamma.*

What becomes evident is that the pantheistic ship comes apart on the reef of evil. One cannot affirm the absence of a self while individualizing *nirvana,* and one cannot talk about the cessation of suffering without also giving the origin of the first wrong thought. Buddhism has an intricate set of rules and regulations because it needs them. As a nontheistic path, it is a road strewn with *kamma.* It recognizes evil and then, fatalistically, shuts its eyes to it, seeking escape.

In striking contrast, the Christian message recognizes the horror of evil and seeks to offer a morally justifiable reason for God to allow suffering. Let us turn to the Christian response, so that we may see the difference.

THE GIVER OF LIFE

When all that the Scriptures have said is pulled together, there are six elements that combine to give an explanation that is coherent and unique. No escape is sought, either in the denial of the question or in the implications of the answer.

First, the God of the Bible reveals Himself as the Author of life and as the Being in whom all goodness dwells. The chasm between the skeptic and the Christian is huge, right from the start. God is not merely good. This means that with reference to God we are dealing with more than moral issues of right and wrong, pleasure or pain. *We are dealing with a transcendent source of goodness that is opted for, not because it is "better" in a hierarchy of options, but because it is the very basis from which all differences are made.* Moral categories, for us, often move in comparisons and hierarchies. We talk in terms of judging or feeling that one thing is better than another. Our culture is more advanced morally than someone else's culture, at least so we may think. God's existence changes those varying categories and moves us not into comparative categories but into a presentation of the very essence of what the word *goodness* is based upon.

God is holy. This difference is what makes the argument almost impossible for a skeptic to grasp. Holiness is not merely goodness. "Why did God not create us to choose only good?" "Why do bad things happen to good people?" The reality is that the opposite of evil, in degree, may be goodness. But the opposite of absolute evil, in kind, is absolute holiness. In the biblical context, the idea of holiness is the tremendous "otherness" of God Himself. God does not just reveal Himself as good; He reveals Himself as holy.

In the play *Phantom of the Opera*, there is a song called "The Music of the Night." It is sung by the half-sinister figure of the Phantom, who woos the woman he loves. He soothes her with his voice and entices her into his world, telling her that the darkness of the night sharpens each sensation and heightens the imagination. He pleads with her to abandon her defenses and yield to the tug of the senses, even as night blankets the eyes of truth.

Then comes this line: "Turn your face away from the garish light of day," because in the darkness, one can change the "oughts" of the conscience to the pleasure of one's passions. The melody is haunting, the words are seductive, and the will is taunted. To such a way of thinking, light *is* garish because it exposes the wickedness that is shrouded by the darkness.

The holiness of God is like light in a dark world. Just as the coming of dawn exposes the thoughts or deeds of the night before and often leaves a sickening feeling of wrong, so holiness discloses what light itself is—the source of discovering and liberating what the lie has ensnared. The Old Testament prophet Isaiah described his awe-stricken state when God revealed Himself to him. Isaiah, a morally good man, nevertheless fell on his face and immediately sensed that he was unfit to be in God's presence. He was not just in the presence of someone better than he was. He was in the presence of the One by whom and because of whom all purity finds its point of reference. That is why he was speechless.

Here, Islam and Christianity do find a partially common perspective. God is transcendent, not only in His being, but in His nature.

God's holiness, in turn, conveys an intrinsic sanctity to our lives. We are His offspring. This is not a culturally conferred sacredness or a legally determined sacredness. Every person has intrinsic value. That value is one's birthright with God as his or her heavenly Father. Was it not that recognition that prompted the question in the first place? If my birth is sacred, then what wrong merited my blindness?

THE SOURCE OF THE STORY

Second, from this authorship flows a deduction. If God is the Author of life, there must be a script. We are not, in Jean Paul Sartre's terms, empty bubbles floating on the sea of nothingness. We are not on a cruise with no purpose or destination or instruments.

It is not that the world is a stage and we can pick and choose different scripts. The lines that are given tell us that this is not a play, but real life that directs the story in every act and thought. The individual subplot must gain its direction from the larger story of God's purpose for our lives.

The blind man, the disciples, and the neighbors all knew the story. In the beginning, God created the heavens and the earth. God was sovereign over every life. How did this man's blindness fit into the story? The particular was seeking an explanation in the larger context. If the larger plot were fully understood, the smaller story would make sense.

There is a very simple way to illustrate this. I referred earlier to a song from Andrew Lloyd Webber's *The Phantom of the Opera,* which has been one of the most successful musicals on Broadway. The music is superb, and the story line is riveting. I recall that when I first heard some of the music over the radio, I was surprised that portions of it seemed discordant, sometimes even shrill. How could the same composer orchestrate both the delightful and the jarring? I could not blend the two until I finally saw the play. Then, it all fit together— the magnificent and the pathetic, the harmony and the discord, the hideous and the beautiful. Why? Because there was a script to explain it.

When one comes to grips with the story of God's plan and purpose born out of His holy and pure character, both good and evil speak within its context. Without God, there is no story, and nothing makes sense.

I once had the privilege to attend a lecture at Cambridge University when Stephen Hawking was speaking. His goal was to examine the question "Is man determined or free?" Hawking went through his material meticulously and then came his long-awaited conclusion: "Is man determined? Yes. But since we do not know what has been determined, we may as well not be."

(I could not resist wondering if he had himself risen above determinism in order to make such a pronouncement, or was the pronouncement part of the determinism he espoused? Had the data encroached upon itself?)

The audience all but groaned. There were actual audible sounds of disappointment. You see, there is no way to understand design without a pattern. There is no right way to live out life if there is no script. In fact, not only do we lose the story, we also lose all commonality of reference for meaning.

During the First World War, something fascinating took place one Christmas Eve. In the midst of an uneasy silence of the guns at night, suddenly a lone voice began to sing a Christmas carol. Irresistibly, another voice joined in, and before one knew it, there was a wave of music because of Bethlehem, cascading across enemy lines, as both sides joined in reading the same script. The story of the babe in a manger, the Prince of Peace, was able to bring communion between warring factions, even for a few hours. This is how a songwriter tells that story. Unfortunately, I can quote only a few stanzas here:

> Oh, my name is Francis Tolliver,
> I come from Liverpool.
> Two years ago the war was waiting
> For me after school,
> From Belgium and to Flanders,
> Germany to here,
> I fought for King and country I love dear.

'Twas Christmas in the trenches
And the frost so bitter hung,
The frozen fields of France were still,
No sounds of peace were sung,
Our families back in England
Were toasting us that day,
Their brave and glorious lads so far away.

I was lying with me mess-mates
On the cold and rocky ground,
When across the lines of battle came
A most peculiar sound.
Says I, "Now listen up, me boys,"
Each soldier strained to hear
As one young German voice rang out so clear.

"He's singing very well, you know,"
My partner says to me.
Soon one by one each German voice joined in the harmony.
The canons rested silent
And the gas cloud rolled no more,
As Christmas brought us respite from the war.

As soon as they were finished
And a reverent pause was spent,
"God Rest Ye Merry Gentlemen"
Struck up some lads from Kent.
The next they sang was "Stille Nacht,"
"Tis 'Silent Night,'" says I,
And in two tongues one song filled up the sky.[10]

You see, two languages can proclaim the same meaning when the message is known to both. When even the thought of God's presence could stop the killing on that night, how much greater impact would the commitment to His entire script have? Goodness can endure a few moments; holiness is life-defining.

God has a script. He has spoken of it in His Scriptures. Finding the script moves us closer to solving the mystery.

THE POINT OF THE STORY

Third, if there is a story, what is at the heart of it? Not only is God holy, but He also reveals to us the *sacred* nature of love, to which He beckons us. And from this sacredness of His love must flow all other loves.

The important aspect of this logical flow is that intrinsic sanctity provides both the reason and the parameters of love. The inability to understand the mystery of evil leads to an inability to understand the sacredness of love. A deadly mistake that I believe our cultures make in the pursuit of meaning is this illusion that love devoid of the sacred, a naked love, is all we need to carry us through life's tests and passions.

Such a love cannot sustain us. Millions of lives are hurt every day in the name of love. Millions of betrayals have been made every day because of love. Love may make the world go round, but it does not keep life straight. In fact, love by itself will make evil more painful. Love can only be what it was meant to be when it is wedded first to the sacred. Sacredness means separateness. Holiness beckons not just to love but moves in increments till it is climaxed in worship.

What does all this have to do with suffering? Everything. You see, when the skeptic asks why God did not fashion us so that we would only choose good, he or she completely misses—drastically misses—what goodness is in God's eyes. Goodness is not an effect. If an effect is all that is important, of course God could make us that way. There is nothing logically contradictory about making us as automatons. But if life is born out of sacredness, neither goodness nor love alone is the goal. It is reverence, and it must be chosen even when it is hard and costly. This kind of love is a choice to let the sanctity of life dictate the commitment of the will. This kind of reverential love can look upon suffering and see it beyond the clutches of time and through the victory of eternity.

Dr. J. Robertson McQuilkin was formerly the president of Columbia Bible College and Seminary. He is one of the most remarkable people in our world. He is a conference speaker and author of note. But none of those credentials exceed his exemplary and heart-gripping love for his ailing wife, Muriel. She has walked down the grim and lonely world of Alzheimer's disease for the last twenty years. Dr. McQuilkin gave up his presidency and numerous other responsibilities to care for her and to love her. He has penned his emotional journey in one of the most magnificent little books ever written. At one point in the book he recounts this incident:

> Once our flight was delayed in Atlanta, and we had to wait a couple of hours. Now that's a challenge. Every few minutes, the same questions, the same answers about what we're doing here, when are we going home? And every few minutes we'd take a fast paced walk down the terminal in earnest search of—what? Muriel had always been a speed walker. I had to jog to keep up with her!
>
> An attractive woman sat across from us, working diligently on her computer. Once, when we returned from an excursion, she said something, without looking up from her papers. Since no one spoke to me or at least mumbled in protest of our constant activity, "Pardon?" I asked.
>
> "Oh," she said, "I was just asking myself, 'Will I ever find a man to love me like that?'"[11]

What a testimony that is to a great love and to a great hunger. Will any one of us find a love, a selfless love like that? We all recognize a sacred love when we see it, and we long for it. Sacred love is not without boundaries. There are lines that commitment will not cross, because when they are crossed it ceases to be love.

Interestingly enough, in the old English usage of words in the wedding ceremony of the Church of England, each spouse standing before the altar pledged to the other, "With my body, I thee worship." That was a remarkable pledge. It meant that there was an exclusivity and reverence physically expressed that gave a language to that love. Until we understand that kind of love we will never understand why it cannot be programmed. Nor, for that matter, will we ever grasp the true nature of evil. From worship flows this love.

That is why God did not make us choose good. It is not goodness we are called to, but worship. Jesus did not just say, "You shall love the Lord your God." He described it as a posture that incorporates mind and heart and soul. When that kind of love is expressed to God, every other love finds its cue.

Robertson McQuilkin ended his book with these words:

> Yet, in her silent world Muriel is so content, so lovable, I sometimes pray, "Please Lord, could you let me keep her a little longer?" If Jesus took her home, how I would miss her gentle sweet presence. Oh yes, there are times when I get irritated, but not often. It doesn't make sense. And besides, I love to care for her. She's my precious.[12]

The book is magnificently titled, *A Promise Kept.* You see, there is a script, and only when that script is etched upon the heart is life truly livable.

Douglas Coupland gives a sobering reflection of a generation, himself included, that wandered in the wilderness of life without God. He cuts through the hype and the velvety veneer of absolute freedom and at the end of his book writes a surprising postscript:

> Now, here is my secret: I tell you with an openness of heart that I doubt I shall ever achieve again, so I pray that you are in a quiet room as you hear these words. My secret is that I need God, that I am sick and can no longer make it alone. I need God to help me give, because I no longer seem to be capable of giving; to help me be kind, as I no longer seem capable of kindness; to help me love, as I seem beyond being able to love.[13]

Only when holiness and worship meet can evil be conquered. For that, only the Christian message has the answer.

THE CENTERPIECE OF THE STORY

This brings us to the fourth step. How is it possible for the sacred to acknowledge the reality of evil and still be able to offer a morally justifiable explanation?

The core of the Christian message posits a way that by all estimates has been a unique and matchless expression in the face of evil. Jesus described His journey to the cross as the very purpose for which He came. His death in that manner brings a message with double force. It demonstrates the destructiveness of evil, which is the cause of suffering and, in Jesus' example, the ability to withstand suffering even though it is undeserved.

Suffering and pain did not spare the very Son of God. Looking at Him on the cross were the very ones who sang songs of joy at His birth. Surely, for Mary, this had to be an utterly traumatic moment. The One who was conceived of God was now at the mercy of man. But I suspect she knew in her heart that something had yet to be completed in the script.

Looking at the cross, evil becomes a mirror of fearsome reality. But by carefully looking *into* the cross, we discover that it is not opaque but translucent, and we are able to glimpse true evil *through* it. The suffering of Jesus is a study in the anatomy of pain. At its core, evil is a challenge of moral proportions against a holy God. It is not merely a struggle with our discomfort. Here, two staggering truths emerge.

Remember what I said as we began, that every exponent seemed to begin with a long list of horrible tragedies or atrocities. Here is the first entailment. The more intense the moral dilemma, the less the skeptic is able to justify it as evil. Alvin Plantinga very cogently points this out for us:

What is genuinely appalling is not suffering as much as human wickedness. But can there be any such thing as horrifying wickedness if naturalism were true? I don't see how. There can be such a thing only if there is a way rational creatures are supposed to live, obliged to live, and the force of normativity is such that appalling and horrifying nature of genuine wickedness is its inverse. Naturalism can perhaps handle foolishness and irrationality, acting contrary to what are your own interests. It can't accommodate appalling wickedness.[14]

The more grim the reality we face, the more obvious is the measuring stick. Though secular thinkers persist in hiding from this truth, we cannot explain appalling wickedness without seeing through it for what it really is.

A few years ago, a rap group recorded a song that became an instant hit. If I were to quote the words here, shock, revulsion, and horror would be the common response. The dehumanizing cruelty, inordinate sadism, and the celebration of violent rape took vulgarity to a new depth of depravity. Yet, within days of its release millions of copies had been bought by anxious fans.

How does one respond to this? Or more to the point, how does one explain it? Was it not witnessing the sadistic delight of the audience in a movie theater as they cheered for cruelty that led the poet William Auden to begin his own search for God? Unvarnished evil bore a terrifying reflection. He was compelled to find an explanation for it.

Where does one look for the explanation? With compelling measure, the cross of Jesus Christ brings into focus evil's assault upon innocence so that we can see both a mirror and a window. How this comes about, I can make but a feeble attempt to explain as we lisp toward clarity. It is here that the second staggering truth emerges.

Eleonore Stump, professor of philosophy at the University of St. Louis, has written an outstanding essay titled, "The Mirror of Evil." Unfolding her own personal journey toward God, she has brought a fascinating argument to the forefront. In the beginning, she recounts Philip Hallie's struggle on the same issue, as he described it in his book *Lest Innocent Blood Be Shed.* Hallie was struggling to work through human depravity. The appalling wickedness that changed his whole life was in coming to terms with the unmitigated brutality in the Nazi death camps. His despair reached its limit when he wrote:

My study of evil incarnate had become a prison whose bars were my bitterness toward the violent, and whose walls were my horrified indifference to mass murder. Between the bars and the walls I revolved like a madman. . . . Over the years I had dug myself into hell.[15]

As he became immersed in this man-made hell, Hallie noticed a hardening in his own heart. He ceased to feel the horror of evil. But as a prisoner to his own indifference, something happened. He came across the heart-gripping work of the people in a small French village, Le Chambon, and found himself responding to their supererogatory acts—acts of extraordinary kindness in the face of evil. Undaunted by the cruelty around them, the Chambonnais repeatedly risked their own lives to rescue those most directly under the Nazi scourge and to alleviate their suffering.

As Hallie read of their deeds of mercy, he found himself almost unconsciously wiping away a tear, then two, then three, till his face was covered with tears. Surprised by such an uncorking of emotion from a heart he thought had died to the schemes of men, he stopped himself and asked, "Why am I crying?"

Had something released him from behind the bars of bitterness and indifference? Had the translucent mirror of evil let through just enough light from the other side that he could see not only the face of wickedness, but also a faint possibility beyond the mirror, the countenance of God? Had some light shone forth from the darkest corner of the world and directed the path of this one, trapped by fear?

On the verge of seeing himself stripped of all feeling in the pit of wickedness, the merciful had opened up a spring of tears. The Chambonnais became a symbol of all that was contrary to the hell unleashed by the Third Reich. There was no more perplexity for him. There was only one antidote. He saw through the wickedness, and Hallie wrote:

We are living in a time, perhaps like every other time, when there are many who, in the words of the prophet Amos, "turn judgment to wormwood." Many are not content to live with the simplicities of the prophet of the ethical plumb line, Amos, when he says in the fifth chapter of his Book, "Seek good, and not evil, that ye may live: and so the Lord, the God of Hosts, shall be with you.". . . . We are afraid to be "taken in," afraid to be credulous, and we are not afraid of the darkness of unbelief about important matters. . . .

But perplexity is a luxury in which I cannot indulge. . . . For me, as for my family, there is the same kind of urgency as far as making ethical judgments is concerned as there were for the Chambonnais when they were making their ethical judgments upon the laws of the Vichy and the Nazis. . . . For me the awareness of the standard of goodness is my awareness of God. I live with the same sentence in my mind that many of the victims of the concentration camps uttered as they walked to their deaths: "Shema Israel, Adonai Elohenu, Adonai Echod." "Hear O Israel, The Lord your God is one."[16]

Borrowing that lesson from Hallie, and thinking of the tear in response to goodness, Eleanor Stump then applies it in her own way. She proves Hallie's point by giving another illustration.

A woman imprisoned for life without parole for killing her husband had her sentence unexpectedly commuted by the governor, and she wept when she heard the news. Why did she cry? Because the news was good, and she had been so used to hearing only bad. But why cry at good news? Perhaps because if most of your news is bad, you need to harden your heart to it. So you become accustomed to bad news, and to one extent or another, you learn to protect yourself against it, maybe by not minding so much. And then good news cracks your heart. It makes it feel keenly again all the evils to which it had become dull. It also opens it up to longing and hope, and hope is painful, because what is hoped for is not yet there. . . .

So, in an odd sort of way, the mirror of evil can also lead us to God. A loathing focus on the evils of our world and ourselves prepares us to be the more startled by the taste of true goodness when we find it and the more determined to follow where it leads. And where it leads is to the truest goodness of all—the goodness of God.[17]

I found this to be surprisingly true in my own life. Just some days ago, I happened to be in Calcutta. It is a city that shows its wounds in public. Some estimates claim up to two million people living on the streets—the old, the young, infants—by the millions, hurting. The pain is so evident and so pervasive that its effect is to anesthetize you against it. Then, with some friends, we visited an orphanage operated by the order founded by Mother Teresa. As we walked in, children rose to their feet in their tiny little beds, and shouts of "Uncle!" came from different parts of the room, as little arms were raised. Our hearts melted, and tears flooded our eyes. Goodness in the face of evil is magnificent, because it is more than goodness; it is the touch of God.

Is this possibly what Malcolm Muggeridge meant when he said:

> Contrary to what might be expected, I look back on experiences that at the time seemed especially desolating and painful, with particular satisfaction. Indeed, I can say with complete truthfulness that everything I have learned in my seventy five years in this world, everything that has truly enhanced and enlightened my existence, has been through affliction and not through happiness, whether pursued or attained. . . . This, of course is what the Cross signifies. And it is the Cross, more than anything else, that has called me inexorably to Christ.[18]

Nobel Laureate Elie Wiesel relates in one of his essays an experience he had when he was a prisoner in Auschwitz. A Jewish prisoner was being executed while the rest of the camp were forced to watch. As the prisoner hung on the gallows—kicking and struggling in the throes of death, refusing to die—an onlooker was heard to mutter under his breath with increasing desperation, "Where is God? Where is He?"

From out of nowhere, Wiesel says, a voice within him spoke to his own heart, saying, "Right there on the gallows; where else?"[19]

Theologian Jurgen Moltmann, commenting on Wiesel's story, astutely observed that any other answer would have been blasphemous.

Is there a more concrete illustration than the death of Christ to substantiate God's presence, right in the midst of pain? He bore the brunt of the pain inflicted by the wickedness of His persecutors—and showed us the heart of God. He displayed in His own suffering what the work of God is all about in changing our hearts from evil to holiness.

In fact, one of the most forgotten realities emerges from the Scriptures. Jesus struggled with the burden of having to be separated from His Father in that momentary event of His crucifixion, as He bore the brunt of evil. He cried out, "My God, My God, why have You forsaken Me?" *The incredible truth was that at the very moment His Father seemed farthest from Him, He was in the center of His Father's will.* That is precisely what an understanding of the cross means. Only when one comes to the cross and sees both in it and beyond it can evil be put in perspective.

What emerges from all of these thoughts is that God conquers *not in spite of the dark mystery of evil, but through it.*

Mahatma Gandhi made the comment that of all the truths of the Christian faith, the one that stood supreme to him was the cross of Jesus. He granted that it was without parallel. It was the innocent dying for the guilty, the pure exchanged for the impure. This evil cannot be understood through the eyes of the ones who crucified Him, but only through the eyes of the Crucified One. *It is the woman who has been raped who understands what rape is, not the rapist. It is the one who has been slandered who understands what slander is, not the slanderer. It is only the One who died for our sin who can explain to us what evil is, not the skeptics.* The cross points the way to a full explanation.

This leads to the "how" of it all.

THE SHOCK OF THE STORY

Fifth, if all that has preceded this is true, then the focus of evil should shift dramatically. Evil is more than an exterior reality that engenders universal suffering; it is an internal reality from which we run.

I recall talking to a very successful and very wealthy businessman who throughout the conversation repeatedly raised this question, "But what about all the evil in this world?" Finally, the friend sitting next to me said to him, "I hear you constantly expressing a desire to see a solution to the problem of evil around you. Are you as troubled by the problem of evil within you?" In the pin-drop silence that followed, the man's face showed his duplicity.

The longer I have encountered this question about evil, the more convinced I am of the disingenuousness of many a questioner. During a forum that I took part in on the subject of evil and suffering, an atheist asked me, "If you found out that God did not exist after all, what would you immediately do that you are not doing now out of fear of Him?"

That, alone, tells you the mind-set. There is a kind of antinomianism—an antilaw state of mind. "If God would get off my back, I could do many more things." One may as well ask, "If there were no policemen to look out for, what kind of speed would you drive?" or, "If there were no criminal justice systems, what kind of crimes would you commit?" or, "If nobody would ever find out, what wickedness would you engage in?" In short, it is a failure to see that the unguarded heart actually makes a prison for everyone—a prison where there are no rules.

Evil is to life what contradiction is to reason. If an argument is contradictory, reasoning breaks down. If life is consumed by evil, life breaks down. The problem of evil begins with me. One of the shortest letters written to an editor was by G. K. Chesterton. It read, "Dear Sir: In response to your article, 'What's wrong with the world'—I am. Yours truly, G. K. Chesterton."

ADMITTING THE SURPRISE

This brings us to our final point in the process of sustaining the Christian world-view regarding evil. The surest evidence that evil is not the enemy of meaning is this inescapable existential reality: that meaninglessness does not come from being weary of pain but from being weary of pleasure. This obvious truth is conspicuously absent in the arguments of skeptics. It is not pain that has driven the West into emptiness; it has been the drowning of meaning in the oceans of our pleasures. Pleasure gone wrong is a greater curse than physical blindness. The blindness to the sacred is the cause of all evil.

This is where Jesus' answer to the question of the blind man comes through with extraordinary power and relevance. When He says that the man's blindness was due neither to the sin of the man nor of his parents but so that the glory of God might be displayed, the lesson is drastic because the message is profound. The restoration of his spiritual sight was indispensable to his understanding of the horror of sin's blindness. Darkness is devastating, and Jesus offers light and life. His cure was to help them see what they were really blind to, yet refused to see.

The problem of evil has ultimately one source. It is the resistance to God's holiness that blanketed all of creation. It is a mystery because we are engulfed in it—spiritual blindness. And there is ultimately only one antidote, the glorious display of God at work within a human soul, bringing about His work of restoration. That transformation tenderizes the heart to become part of the solution and not part of the problem. Such a transformation begins at the cross.

But like the skeptics of Jesus' day, some want to find a reason to deny who Christ is and the healing He can bring. Like the neighbors, the curious masses wish to know how it happened. Like the parents, those who come into close contact will witness the transformation that Christ brings. And like the blind man, those who have personally experienced Christ's power to transform their lives will understand the greater blindness from which they have been rescued.

This may be the real-life illustration in the struggle of which Mark Triplett wrote with such candor. The truth is not that his suffering and pain were brought about by the death of his son and his fear that he had caused it. As he himself had realized, by the terrible scourge of profaning the sacred, he had already brought about a separation from God and suffering to his own soul. He recognized what it had done to him—he had betrayed his wife, betrayed his family, and betrayed his God. The purveyors of sensual pleasure knew full well that his insatiable involvement with their offerings would take him down the road to financial waste and the potential death of his marriage. In the name of pleasure, they had inflicted the ultimate pain. Everything of worth was lost.

Here, at least, one man was stopped in his tracks to understand the cause and effect in a way that the skeptic never seems to understand. Whether or not the father's sin had taken the son's life is not the real point. In fact, the truth is that when Mark uttered those angry words to God, Adam was already dead. What is now pertinent is that through the loss of his son's life, the father has been brought face to face with what was killing him on the inside. But in the midst of that tragedy, the work of God was displayed. He procured pleasures of infinitely greater value than the profane pleasures of excitement without worth and without promise. The embrace of a forgiving wife, the lasting impact of a departed son, the fresh commitment to life's sacred trusts—these are the real treasures of life. That which had snared him was suddenly nauseating and repugnant to him. That to which he is now freed is to tell the world that life's real worth is to be found only in God.

When God restores our spiritual sight through the mystery of evil, we are then able to see the work of God displayed within the framework of our most difficult question. With tears of joy we bend before Him.

In summary, for the Christian, evil is real, this world is real, and time is real. Jesus recognized all three realities with reference to the blind man. He pointed out that this world has built into it the component of time. And upon the anvil of time beats the hammer of eternity until time ultimately reflects the values of the eternal and will be shed as a shell, from within which ultimate truths will be freely embraced. When we enter that stage, we will find out that the real anvil was eternity, that time provided the hammers, and that God's glory and purpose will be what remains.

Chapter Six
WHEN GOD WAS SILENT

IN ROBERT BOLT'S PLAY BASED ON THE LIFE OF SIR THOMAS MORE, *A Man for All Seasons,* there is an incredibly poignant moment when More is brought before a makeshift court. The judge and jury are enraged because he will not side with their spineless scheme to support the king in his immoral decision.

Mounting the threat of death, they pressure More to join their ranks. But he stands quietly before them, refusing to acquiesce. They know very well the reason for his wordless response, but they continue to ply and bully, all in an effort to make him break his silence and speak. Still, More says nothing.

At one point, one of the judges says to him, "Your silence must then be construed as a denial of the affirmation we seek, because that is what the people will take it to mean."

Sir Thomas More, in measured words, replies, "The world must construe according to its wits. This court must construe according to the law."

They finally give up. They cannot break him. But he pays for his commitment to truth with his life.

It is with good reason that some of the finest novelists and playwrights have dug their narrative spades into the soil of injustice. Philosophers from the time of Socrates and Plato have placed supreme value in the virtue of justice in any civilized society. Aristotle went so far as to say that justice was the cornerstone of all ethics. Why? Because justice is the handmaiden of truth, and when truth dies, justice is buried with it. The silence that attends such a tragedy may well be the silence accorded the perpetrators, a haunting moment of truth.

Thomas More probably saw his precedent in Jesus, who stood before a similar court as He was being charged with, among other things, treason against the king. As Jesus stood before Pontius Pilate and those who accused Him, His demeanor was fascinating. His silence was nerve-racking to His questioners. They were hoping that in a war of words they could subdue Him. It was not by accident that their conversation, supposedly dealing with justice, actually ended up in a discussion of truth.

The sequence of events that brought Jesus before Pilate shows how organized crime also has an ancient legacy. Cowardice, treachery, falsehood, scheming, murder—all the passions that authors of fiction draw upon in their suspense novels—spring to life in the harsh reality of the most historic display of injustice in history, when truth was on trial.

The religious leaders wanted Jesus out of their way. But they were torn between two systems of law—their own and the laws of Rome. Try as they would, they could engineer no moral grounds on which to kill Jesus. But even if they could have constructed some scenario of moral justification, they did not have the authority to execute Him, which was their intended goal. It often happens that when the moral law protects the innocent, a ceremonial law is invoked to accomplish immoral ends.

Jesus committed an unpardonable offense in their eyes when He claimed to be equal with God. That, of course, carried no weight in a Roman court, as long as He did not pose a threat to Caesar. In the Greco-Roman world, it is said, to the popular mind all religions were considered to be equally true; to the philosophers, they were equally false; and to the magistrates, they were equally useful.

In short, Rome was no friend to Hebrew religion. The only hope of the high priest and his party, therefore, was to argue their case by representing Jesus' crime as a challenge to Caesar and a crime of treason. They no more cared for Caesar's well-being than Caesar cared for theirs. But the ploy helped their case.

Caught in the middle of all this was the weak-kneed Roman governor,

Pontius Pilate. Old Testament scholar Dennis Kinlaw has astutely noted that poor old Mrs. Pilate never envisioned that her son's name would make it across history—etched into the Christian creeds. No doubt, he, himself, never gave thought to the momentous trial that would be permanently scripted into the story of civilization.

With all that Jesus said to Pilate, Pilate marveled most at His silence. The Bible says, "The chief priests accused him of many things. So again Pilate asked him, 'Aren't you going to answer? See how many things they are accusing you of.' But Jesus still made no reply, and Pilate was amazed" (Mark 15:3–5).

The interaction between them gives us a critical look at how Jesus handled the skeptic's taunt and the religious person's anger at Him. Jesus had already been through an exhausting series of events. First, He had been arrested when Judas sold out for a meager sum of money and took Him to Annas, the father-in-law of the high priest, Caiaphas. After questioning Him, Annas sent Him on to Caiaphas, who shrewdly sought to justify a crucifixion by quoting Scripture, that it was imperative that "one die for the many."

Caiaphas, in turn, sent him to Pilate who, unknown to the priest, had been warned by his wife not to incriminate himself in this horrible plot. Discovering that Jesus was a Galilean, Pilate wrested an excuse to avoid making a judgment and sent Him to King Herod. But Pilate could not avoid his appointment with destiny. For Herod, after taunting Jesus, sent Him back to Pilate.

Jesus became an object flung from one set of hands to the other, as words and intentions were woven together to subvert the truth, all in the name of morality. When Pilate finished examining Him, he said to the religious authorities, "You brought me this man as one who was inciting the people to rebellion. I have examined him in your presence and have found no basis for your charges against him. Neither has Herod, for he sent him back to us; as you can see, he has done nothing to deserve death. Therefore, I will punish him and then release him" (Luke 23:14–16). And Pilate had Him flogged, in an attempt to somehow appease the crowd.

This was the moment the leaders of the synagogue had awaited, and in the will of God, this was the moment toward which all of history had been moving and by which history would be forevermore defined. There is much that can be said here, but it is Jesus' conversation with Pilate that occupies our attention.

THE OPENING LINES

The text, as we study it, does not begin with Jesus' silence. It begins with a brief interchange between Jesus and Pilate before Jesus refused to answer some of Pilate's questions. We would be prudent, therefore, if we first look at the answers He did give, because His silence is understood in the light of the words He spoke.

The first question Pilate asked Jesus was very straightforward: "Are You the king of the Jews?"

This was a specifically worded question. Pilate would have preferred to keep it an internal affair between the Jews. That way, he might possibly have been able to avoid any responsibility in the matter. The priests, on the other hand, knew they would have to drag Rome into the problem if they were to have the legal authority to execute Jesus. With these cross-purposes, the trial began.

To the question from Pilate about His kingship, Jesus countered with a question of His own: "Is that your own idea, or did others talk to you about Me?"

Pilate snapped back, "Am I a Jew? It was *Your* people and *Your* chief priests who handed You over to me. What is it You have done?" (see John 18:33–35).

Pilate was evidently irritated by Jesus' question, but he had obviously missed the point. What Jesus wanted to expose to Pilate was the concealed disingenuousness that lay behind his question—mere ceremonial curiosity. To answer a question for which an answer is not genuinely sought is only to prolong the charade. Jesus was closing in on Pilate to show him that he was really no different from those who were bringing the accusation against Him. The significance of this question is that the confrontation did not pertain only to one nation of people. This implicated the whole world. His accusers were willfully deaf to His answers, even as Pilate was performing a function of his office with complete disregard for truth behind his judgments. God was on the witness stand; humanity was playing its courtroom shenanigans.

An immediate lesson surfaces. We hear so much criticism from skeptics about what they often brand as "secondhand faith." It is implied that many people believe in God only because of the context of their birth or family or determined conditions. If the criticism is justified, and undoubtedly it sometimes is, why do we not show the same distrust of secondhand doubt? If it is possible for a person's belief to be merely an echo of someone else's faith, are there not hypocrites in doubt also?

Was this a genuine search on the part of this Roman governor, or was it the pretense of a procedure, reflecting no real will to listen? That was Jesus' point.

I have, on numerous occasions, heard some valiant questioner pile argument upon argument to challenge the Christian faith. The arguments begin to sound hollow when you recognize by the very wording that they are the expressions of another's voice or borrowed from some notable thinker. This is not to suggest the validity or the invalidity of the question or of the argument. This is only to assert that, many times, so-called reasons for rejecting the truth are so blended with individual prejudice that it is hard to differentiate between the question and the wanton desire of the questioner.

Some time ago, I was lecturing at a university on the assigned subject, "Ethics and the Invasion of Cyberspace." I was told that I was invited as the token theist so that there would be at least one speaker who would propose a transcendent basis for ethical judgments! It was a fascinating conference.

After the lecture, we sat down together for a lunch hosted by faculty members and student leaders. During the lunch, one of the faculty members said something like this: "All this philosophizing about an objective morality seems so highbrow and philosophically weighty. The basic question I have is very simple: How do we keep students from cheating?"

As I answered her question, I also reminded her that she was still dealing with the symptoms and ignoring the cause.

At the end of the lunch, a handful of students surrounded me with a flurry of questions. One of them, in low tones, said, "I really have a problem. I was asked by my professor to come and take in your lecture and to critique what you said. But the truth is that after hearing your arguments, I find myself agreeing with you."

"Well, then," I asked, "why don't you say that in your paper?"

"Oh no! I will be definitely docked in my grades if I concur with your reasoning. The professor had been certain that I would disagree with you and wanted me to offer a scathing rebuttal. I am a straight-A student, and I cannot afford to drop my grade."

"Are you sure your professor will penalize you just for agreeing with this position on ethics?" I asked her.

"I am positive," she said.

"Was your professor here at the luncheon?" I asked.

"Yes," came the obviously hesitant response.

"Who was it?"

There was an awkward silence and then an even more uncomfortable admission. "The one who asked you how she could keep students from cheating."

So much for the genuine hunger for truthfulness. I seriously had to wonder if a teacher such as that really wanted her students to learn not to cheat or only to learn to think as she did, even if it meant an entire life of pretense—secondhand doubt.

I am convinced that there are tens of thousands of students turned out of our universities whose minds have been trained to disbelieve in God, any contrary argument or evidence notwithstanding. The father of modern rationalism is the French philosopher Rene Descartes. His dictum—"I think, therefore I am"—resonates in the halls of philosophy. From that fundamentally rationalistic approach to existence, skeptics have extrapolated their own dictum—"I doubt, therefore I am an intellectual." For many, such doubting actually follows a particular intellectual, rather than squarely facing the questions of the intellect.

A DIFFERENT KING

Jesus was well aware of the contagion of doubt. That, in part, was His reason for remaining quiet. Pilate, of course, quickly dismissed any personal involvement in the proceedings by insisting that it was an internal matter within the Jewish community that had started the whole problem in the first

place. Jesus then proceeded to pursue Pilate to the point that he would
ize that it indeed *was* Pilate's concern, because Jesus' kingship did not ha
anything to do with the governance of a nation or of a culture, but had *everything* to do with the rule of the heart.

Jesus said, "My kingdom is not of this world. If it were, my servants would
fight to prevent my arrest by the Jews. But now my kingdom is from another
place" (John 18:36).

Pilate, somewhat taken aback, exclaimed, "You are a king, then!"

This was when the defining answer came. "You are right in saying I am a
king. In fact, for this reason I was born, and for this I came into the world,
to testify to the truth. Everyone on the side of truth listens to me" (v. 37).

Immediately, we notice that three dramatic assertions have been made.

First, that Jesus' kingdom was of such a nature that it was not procured by
military might or power. Its rule is neither territorial nor political. If history
has proven anything, it is that the spread of the gospel by the sword or by
coercion has done nothing but misrepresent the message and bring disrepute
to the gospel.

To be sure, Jesus was not talking here about pacifism or warfare. He was
making a definite difference between the way His kingdom grows and the way
earthly nations establish control. He was making a significant point to a pros-
ecutor with political motives. His kingship cannot and will not be established
by force or threat. This fact alone would have given Pilate reason enough to go
beyond the surface of what was going on. It was really the nations of this world
that were on the witness stand, and God who was doing the judging. Pilate
ought to have known immediately that this was no Caesar standing in front of
him. This was someone with a drastically different kind of authority.

At the risk of repetition, at this point I would like to recount an instance
I have shared in some of my other writings. I do so now because I wish to
carry this a step further.

Some years ago, a military general in Russia invited me to speak at a
round-table discussion with seven members of the faculty who chaired different departments at the Center for Geo-Political Strategy in Moscow. From
the beginning, the atmosphere in the room was cold and antagonistic and

their faces hard. One by one, their attacks came upon
nd upon Christianity in particular with its history
I attempted to defuse one question after another but
cussion was progressing nowhere because they kept
Christendom's checkered past.

We suddenly came to a very tense moment. One of the officers, with great passion and antagonism in his voice, leaned toward me and said, "I remember as a child seeing a German soldier come into my home and shoot my grandmother to death. On his belt buckle were the words, 'God is for us.' *That* is what religion has done for our country!" he charged.

He was right. Perhaps he did not remember, or even know, that those buckles were not thus inscribed by the Nazis, but were remnant paraphernalia from the days of the Kaiser. As the Nazi war machine ground down into a serious lack of equipment, they had begun to use these remnants from a bygone era. That aside, from the days of Constantine, the symbol of the cross has been so repeatedly emblazoned on weapons of hatred and war that the message of Christ has been apprehended by what Nietzsche called "the will to power."

I paused and admitted to him that I partially agreed with what he had said.

That surprised him, and he cautiously lowered his guard. Then I said this: "But you know, General, Jesus never came to establish a government upon the people by force. He did not even talk about political systems. He came to rule in the hearts of people, and not by the establishment of political power. He asks to live in *you*, not to control your state."

With that, I went on to share my own personal testimony with them. I was on the verge of quoting what Aleksander Solzhenitsyn once said, that the thin line between good and evil does not run through states or ideologies, but through the heart of every man and woman. But I resisted, fearing that even that reference may have stirred political passion.

The officers were very quiet when I finished, some looking introspective and others reluctantly nodding their heads in agreement. The general who had invited me had a look of calm triumph over his face, as if to say, "There, gentlemen, is the answer you and I never thought of."

I then went on to ask them what seventy years of Marxism had done for their people. I reminded them of the emptiness in the lives of their youth, who were now living in one of the most lawless countries on earth.

As suddenly as the subject had been introduced in the first place, so dramatically did the tenor of the conversation change. It is ironic, I think, that the city of Moscow bears the scars of the brutality of both Nazism and Napoleon's exploits. There are reminders of what the Nazis did and markers of how far Napoleon came in his attempt to defeat Russia. Their names symbolize terror and war to the huge Soviet Empire. The still-vivid memories of their savageries make the Russian people ever skeptical of any power that threatens.

Yet, in an extraordinarily staggering statement about Jesus Christ, Napoleon said something that is almost unexcelled by any political leader. I quote it at length because of its incredible insight. I only wish I had had it with me when I met with these generals. Napoleon expressed these thoughts while he was exiled on the rock of St. Helena. There, the conqueror of civilized Europe had time to reflect on the measure of his accomplishments. He called Count Montholon to his side and asked him, "Can you tell me who Jesus Christ was?" The count declined to respond. Napoleon countered:

 Well then, I will tell you. Alexander, Caesar, Charlemagne and I myself have founded great empires; but upon what did these creations of our genius depend? Upon force. Jesus alone founded His empire upon love, and to this very day millions will die for Him. . . . I think I understand something of human nature; and I tell you, all these were men, and I am a man: none else is like Him; Jesus Christ was more than man. . . . I have inspired multitudes with such an enthusiastic devotion that they would have died for me . . . but to do this it was necessary that I should be visibly present with the electric influence of my looks, my words, of my voice. When I saw men and spoke to them, I lighted up the flame of self-devotion in their hearts. . . . Christ alone has succeeded in so raising the mind of man toward the unseen, that it becomes insensible to the barriers of time and space. Across a chasm of eighteen hundred years, Jesus Christ makes a demand which is beyond all others difficult to satisfy; He asks for that which a philosopher may often seek in vain at the hands of his friends, or a father of his children, or a bride of her spouse, or a man of his brother. He asks for the human heart; He will have it entirely to Himself. He demands it unconditionally; and forthwith His demand is granted. Wonderful! In defiance of time and space, the soul of man, with all its powers and faculties, becomes an annexation to the empire of Christ. All who sincerely believe in Him, experience that remarkable, supernatural love toward Him. This phenomenon is unaccountable; it is altogether beyond the scope of man's creative powers. Time, the great destroyer, is powerless to extinguish this sacred flame; time can neither exhaust its strength nor put a limit to its range. This is it, which strikes me most; I have often thought of it. This it is which proves to me quite convincingly the Divinity of Jesus Christ.[1]

Whatever else one may say in response, it is difficult to explain this away as mere eloquence. In fact, it was to counter mere eloquence and such artificial power that Napoleon said what he did. With unbelievable insight, he saw how Jesus Christ conquered. It was not by force, but by winning the heart.

Napoleon understood Jesus better than Pilate did. Pilate probably had no clue what Jesus meant when He said, "My kingdom is not of this world," or how far into the future this Christ would conquer—and that, without the methods by which empires are normally expanded, of which Rome was a prime example.

A DIFFERENT CAUSE

Having given the first part of His answer, Jesus moves to the second. "For this reason I was born, and for this I came into the world, to testify to the truth. Everyone on the side of truth listens to me" (John 18:37).

This is one of the most defining statements Jesus ever made, both for His mission and for our ultimate condition. His purpose in coming was to testify to the truth. He already knew who He was. His testimony was to reveal to us who *we* are. His answers would not change under any pressure His accusers could apply. Whenever He spoke, He spoke the truth. His word was truth.

This conversation could have placed Pilate in a very unique place in history, on the side of that which was right, had he only asked his question and waited for the answer. Instead, in dramatic fashion, he responded to Jesus' statement that anyone who is on the side of truth listens to Him with an impatient dismissal, "What is truth?" and walked away. He did not wait for the answer and so proved Jesus' point that he was not really looking for the truth.

Pilate walked out of the hall abruptly and tried to set Jesus free. He just wanted out of the whole situation. He offered the crowd a choice. He would free a prisoner of their choosing, any prisoner, because it was Passover time. He hoped and probably felt sure that they would opt for the release of Jesus. But he was out of step with the determination of the religious leaders. Instead of calling for Jesus' release they cried for Barabbas, who had been imprisoned because of his part in a political rebellion. That itself showed that it was not Jesus' rebellion against Rome that prompted their motive; rather, it was their rebellion against God that was impelling their passions. This is how the Bible tells the story, as recorded in John 19:4–7:

> Once more Pilate came out and said to the Jews, "Look, I am bringing him out to you to let you know that I find no basis for a charge against him." When Jesus came out wearing the crown of thorns and the purple robe, Pilate said to them, "Here is the man!"
>
> As soon as the chief priests and their officials saw him, they shouted, "Crucify! Crucify!"
>
> But Pilate answered, "You take him and crucify him. As for me, I find no basis for a charge against him."
>
> The Jews insisted, "We have a law, and according to that law he must die, because he claimed to be the Son of God."

The Bible then adds this:

> When Pilate heard this, he was even more afraid, and he went back inside the palace. "Where do you come from?" he asked Jesus, but Jesus gave him no answer. "Do you refuse to speak to me?" Pilate said. "Don't you realize I have power either to free you or to crucify you?"
>
> Jesus answered, "You would have no power over me if it were not given to you

from above. Therefore the one who handed me over to you is guilty of a greater sin." (John 19:8–11)

Finally, Pilate handed Him over to be crucified.

In many ways Pilate is a most pitiable character, for he lived in fear on every side. He feared Caesar, if perchance he conveyed that he did not deal with someone who was a threat to Rome. He feared the implications of what he was doing, because his wife had warned him that she had had a dream about Jesus and that he should not have a share in punishing that innocent man. He feared Jesus Himself, not quite sure who he was dealing with.

Pilate may well be the quintessential example of what politics has come to mean. He knew what was right but succumbed to the seduction of his position. In life's most severe tests of motives, there is a politician in each and every one of us. While Pilate was ignorant of the role he was playing, the priests justified their heinous deed, quoting Scripture in support of their cause. Divine purpose, political maneuvering, and religious fervor met in the plan of redemption.

It was to be God's Passover Lamb that Jesus came into the world in the first place. The world wanted to explain Him away by its own wits. He stood at the bar of God's grace and spoke mercy. It was at this point that the Lamb of God began to move to the moment of death.

There are four distinct references to Jesus' silence along this trail to His death. Let us probe them.

The first occurs when He is standing before the Sanhedrin, as narrated in Mark 14:60. Conflicting testimony was given by false witnesses. Their charges did not add up, yet Jesus remained silent. Contradiction itself ought to be self-indicting. When it is not, either truth or truthfulness has died.

The second silence occurred when, in the presence of Pilate, the high priests repeated their charges of treason, and Jesus remained silent. He knew that they were determined to crucify Him. It is difficult to bring a defense against religion without truth, especially when it is galvanized by a crowd. Any words of self-defense on Jesus' part would have been pointless.

I believe that Jesus' demeanor here is profoundly exemplary. It was the silence of truth in the midst of the noise of prejudice and hate. I have personally experienced situations like this and have witnessed others in a similar position. The one who stands silently in the face of mocking and hate-filled people exposes the scandalous capacity of hatred and, in his silence, speaks volumes of God's character.

The third moment of silence is in front of Herod and his band of mockers. They wanted a show. The Bible says this:

> When Herod saw Jesus, he was greatly pleased, because for a long time he had been wanting to see him. From what he had heard about him, he hoped to see him perform some miracle. He plied him with many questions, but Jesus gave him no answer. . . .
>
> Then Herod and his soldiers ridiculed and mocked him. Dressing him in an elegant robe, they sent him back to Pilate. That day Herod and Pilate became friends—before this they had been enemies. (Luke 23:8–9, 11–12)

This passage tells a fearsome tale. There are many who want Jesus to be nothing more than a miracle worker or an entertainer. And how ironic it is that enemies became friends out of a common desire to be rid of Him. Has anything changed since then?

The fourth time Jesus was silent was when Pilate became fearful, hearing that He claimed to be the Son of God. "Where do You come from?" he asked. But Jesus remained silent. He had already told Pilate where He came from. But Pilate did not have the courage to deal with His answer.

In the mix of these silent responses, there is a wealth of thought from God to us.

A DIFFERENT POWER

First, there is the silence of *goodness* in the face of orchestrated evil. The entire episode before the Sanhedrin was an effort to frame Him. They knew their power. He knew their weakness. They knew the letter of the law. He knew the spirit of the moral code. They did not know Him. He knew them.

Anytime evil becomes organized, its ferocity breathes the air of hell. There is nothing that can quench that fury. It cannot be stopped until it has accomplished its purpose. That is why hell is unending. Its nature is to burn on the inside, and no outward consolation or influence can change wickedness that is inflamed by numbers.

The second silence is the silence of *perception*. When evil justifies itself by posturing as morality, God becomes the devil and the devil, God. That exchange makes one impervious to reason. Certainly, the high priests represented that lot. Nothing, absolutely nothing that Jesus could have said would have convinced them of who He really was or caused them even to care. Their capacity to hate and their love for ceremonial law far exceeded any desire to know truth and goodness.

Jesus knew that their love for the law was nothing more than a desire to find ways to manipulate the law to serve their own immoral ends. Anytime Scripture is quoted for the express purpose of advancing one's selfish aims, light is turned into darkness.

In all of literature, there are very few passages that are as gripping and penetrating in insight as Dostoevsky's portrayal of the Grand Inquisitor in his book *Brothers Karamazov*. In a conversation with his younger brother, Alyosha, who was far more spiritually minded than he, Ivan, an atheist, is relating of a time when he, too, thought on spiritual matters. In fact, he had even penned a poem that he called "The Grand Inquisitor." It was the title Ivan had given to an aged chief cardinal heading the Spanish Inquisition. Alyosha asked Ivan to tell him about the poem, and Ivan narrated it as prose. It was based on events during the 1500s, in the Spanish town of Seville, when the Church was burning "heretics" at the stake. After giving the historical backdrop, Ivan began his story.

On a certain day that a large number of heretics had been tortured and burned under the complete and angry command of the Grand Inquisitor, suddenly, in the midst of all the appalling sounds and sights of torture, a figure quietly and gently appeared and walked among the suffering.

He came softly, unobserved, and yet, strange to say, everyone recognized Him. . . . The people are irresistibly drawn to Him, they surround Him, they flock about Him, follow Him. The sun of love burns in His heart, light and power shine from His eyes, and their radiance, shed on people, stirs their hearts with responsive love.

It is obvious that in Ivan's narration this figure is Jesus Christ, walking in simple guise among the people. Suddenly, the Grand Inquisitor came along in his carriage and saw Him. Recognizing who He was, he immediately had Him arrested and thrown into prison. That night, lantern in hand, in his coarse cassock, he came to visit his prisoner. The conversation is profound:

"Is it Thou? Thou?" But receiving no answer, he added at once, "Don't answer, be silent. What canst Thou say, indeed? I know too well what Thou wouldst say. And Thou hast no right to add anything to what Thou hadst said of old. Why, then, art Thou come to hinder us? For Thou hast come to hinder us, and Thou knowest that. But dost Thou know what will be tomorrow? . . . I shall condemn Thee and burn Thee at the stake as the worst of heretics. And the very people who have kissed Thy feet, to-morrow at the faintest sign from me will rush to heap up the embers of Thy fire. . . ."

When the inquisitor ceased speaking he waited some time for his prisoner to answer him. His silence weighed down upon him. He saw that the prisoner had listened intently all the time, looking gently in his face and evidently not wishing to reply. The old man longed for Him to say something, however bitter and terrible. But He suddenly approached the old man in silence and softly kissed him on his bloodless lips. That was all His answer. The old man shuddered. His lips moved. He went to the door, opened it, and said to Him: "Go, and come no more. . . . Come not at all, never, never!" And he let Him out into the dark alleys of town.[2]

Dostoevsky's genius reveals a brilliant understanding of the power of miracle, mystery, and authority. The Inquisitor lives in many a religious person's mind even today. We scream at Jesus but want no answer that will add to the claims He has already made. We want Him to leave and come no more.

Such was the mind-set of the religious authorities. Jesus' silence was purposeful. He knew what His questioners were about.

But His silence was not only one of character and perception, it was also the silence of *consistency*. By His silence He taught us how to fight slander. His behavior was in keeping with His teaching. This, over the years, has come home to me as possibly one of the most easily missed examples that Jesus set for us in the face of so much that was reprehensible in human behavior. His silence is a lesson that answers are not always the way to reason. To give in to the temptation to try to fight slander with words in most instances dirties both the slanderer and the one who has been slandered. Escaping from slander, therefore, is a hazardous task when the very accusation can become valid not because of the truth, but because of the lack of composure with which one seeks to defend oneself. Jesus made no such mistake.

I have been told of an incident that occurred some years ago. As I was not present, I was not privy to the details. But the same descriptions of the event came to me from several different sources. A Christian leader was being subjected to the haranguing and bullying of some in the church who wanted him out. There was no big killer argument that could be mounted. So petty and ridiculous charges were made with unmasked fury, leveled one after another.

To a person, the identical report came back that the most eloquent expression of the entire occasion was the example of the leader, who sat silently before his accusers with tears staining his face. He had nothing to say and yet, everything was communicated. The outbursts and the tirades of the attackers were nothing less than the poisonous venom of misguided lives. Such scenarios ought to be instructive of true power. The man who was the one accused looked like Christ in the midst of his enemies.

But finally, we must understand that the silence of Jesus was the silence of *fulfilled mission*. His silence before those who were to take His life was predicted by the prophet Isaiah, eight hundred years before it took place: "He was oppressed and afflicted, yet he did not open his mouth; he was led like a lamb to the slaughter, and as a sheep before her shearers is silent, so he did not open his mouth" (Isa. 53:7).

It is a natural reaction to speak in our own defense, even when we are in the wrong. He remained silent, though He was innocent of the charges. His silence was for our sake, because He stands before the Father on our behalf.

At the heart of this entire episode is a truth that God had given from before the foundation of the world.

In *The Lion, the Witch and the Wardrobe*, C. S. Lewis wrote a magnificent passage illustrating this. Aslan, the lion, is a figure of Christ. One of the children, Edmond, had betrayed Aslan and endangered his siblings by selling out to the wicked witch, the Queen of Narnia, who had seduced him by offering him a taste of turkish delight. By the terms of the law, that betrayal merited Edmond's death. There was only one way to save Edmund: Aslan must be delivered into the hands of the queen, which had been the real objective in her scheme all alone.

Quietly and without resistance, the more powerful Aslan submits to the queen's demands. After he was humiliated, he was bound to a table of stone, which represented the law, and killed. Edmond's sisters, Lucy and Susan, were totally despondent as they grieved over their friend. Suddenly, Aslan appeared before them, triumphant over death. "What does it all mean?" they wondered. Lewis, at this point in the story, makes this brilliant observation.

"It means," said Aslan, "that though the Witch knew the Deep Magic, there is a magic deeper still which she did not know. Her knowledge only goes back to the dawn of Time. But if she could have looked a little further back, into the stillness and the darkness before Time dawned, she would have read there a different incantation. She would have known that when a willing victim who had committed no treachery was killed in a traitor's stead, the Table would crack and Death itself would start working backwards."[3]

That incantation that Lewis speaks of is the prior will of God, that He who knew no sin would willingly lay down His life to pay the price of sin. The Word of God, as promised, was fulfilled.

A DIFFERENT WAY

Does Jesus' silence, with all of the implications that we have drawn, reveal a contrast to others in similar situations who have claimed divine or prophetic status?

Yes, it does. Dramatically so. He came with a message and a method that address three very significant differences on individuality and society. I speak of conversion, compulsion, and revelation. How is the Christian faith unique?

First is the issue of conversion. Jesus' message reveals that every individual, whether Jew or Greek or Roman or from any other civilization, comes to know God not by virtue of birth, but by a conscious choice to let Him have His rule in his or her individual life. Jesus' kingdom is not of this world, neither is our inheritance in His kingdom a world into which we enter by physical birth.

This is very important to understand. We are living in a time when angry voices demand with increasing insistence that we ought not to propagate the gospel, that we ought not to consider anyone "lost" just because they are not "Christians." "We are all born into different beliefs, and therefore, we should leave it that way"—so goes the tolerant "wisdom" of our time. Mahatma Gandhi, for example, strongly spoke out against the idea of conversion. When people make such statements, they forget or don't know that *nobody* is born a Christian. All Christians are such by virtue of conversion. To ask the Christian not to reach out to anyone else who is from another faith is to ask that Christian to deny his own faith.

One of India's leading "saints," Sri Ramakrishna, is said to have been for a little while a Muslim, for a little while a Christian, and then finally, a Hindu again, because he came to the conclusion that they are all the same. If they are all the same, why did he revert to Hinduism? It is just not true that all religions are the same. Even Hinduism is not the same within itself. Thus, to deny the Christian the privilege of propagation is to propagate to him or her the fundamental beliefs of another religion.

If conversion is individual and not by virtue of birth, this leads us to the next issue of compulsion. The teaching of Jesus is clear. No one ought to be compelled to become a Christian. This sets the Christian faith drastically apart from Islam. In no country where the Christian faith is the faith of the majority is it illegal to propagate another faith. There is no country in the world that I know of where the renunciation of one's Christian faith puts one in danger of being hunted down by the powers of state. Yet, there are numerous Islamic countries where it is against the law to publicly proclaim the gospel of Jesus

Christ, and where a Muslim who renounces his or her belief in Islam to believe in anything else risks death. Freedom to critique the text of the Koran and the person of Mohammed are prohibited by the laws of blasphemy, and the result is torturous punishment. One must respect the concern of a culture to protect what it deems sacred, but to compel a belief in Jesus Christ is foreign to the gospel, and that is a vital difference. The contrast is all too clear.

It is in this matter of conversion and compulsion that political theory emerges. As I stated earlier, the gospel is not to be spread at the point of a sword. When Christendom has resorted to such methods, it was not the gospel of Jesus Christ that was propagated, but a political theory that used the gospel for the benefit of power-seeking institutions and individuals. People are justifiably fearful when they think of religion in tandem with political control. Jesus' method was to touch the heart of the individual so that he or she responded to Him out of love for Him, rather than from compulsion or control.

Contrast this with the practice of Mohammed. However one might wish to interpret it, the sword and warfare are an intrinsic part of the Islamic faith. Even the best of apologists for Islam acknowledge the use of the sword in Islam but will mitigate it by saying that in each instance it was for defensive purposes. I suggest that the reader read the Koran and the history of Islam for himself to determine whether this was so.

As for the executions that were carried out at Mohammed's behest, his apologists argue that they were not so much ordered by him as carried out on his behalf. Here again, I would recommend reading the narrative to see if this defense is in keeping with the historic record.

But even the best of Muslim apologists is hard-pressed to navigate around Mohammed's own injunction to kill, illustrated in a verse from the Koran known as the *ayatus-saif,* or "the verse of the sword."

> But when the forbidden months are past, then fight and slay the idolaters wherever ye find them, and take them, and prepare for them each ambush. But if they repent and establish worship and pay the poor due, then leave their way free. (Surah 9.5)

One Islamic scholar takes off on this passage and makes this comment:

And a traitor guilty of high treason is an outlaw and may be killed by anyone without any special authority. May God guide us all to the Truth and spread peace and unity amongst mankind![4]

I shall say no more on this very difficult and divisive issue here because any comment would breed hard feelings, and that is not my desire. What it clearly boils down to is this. Where Islam and Christianity do agree is that truth is supreme; however, they see truth finally revealed in different persons—in Islam through Mohammed, and in Christianity through Jesus Christ. This is why a comparison between the two persons is necessary.

This brings us to the final matter. At the heart of all this lies one issue. Jesus' silence does not mean He does not speak. He reminds us that He has already spoken in His Word, the Scriptures. Here, the final source of authority is truly divergent from other faiths.

The Muslim sees the Koran as the perfect and final revelation of Allah. Allah was the revealer, and Mohammed was the receptor. The very words were dictated to him. He, to them, is the last and the greatest prophet. The proof of his supremacy is the beauty of the Koran. It is the *book* that is considered to be the ultimate expression of perfection and the repository of truth.

The difficulty here is manifold. How does one sustain that this written text is perfect? Let us consider just one troublesome aspect, the grammatical flaws that have been demonstrated. Ali Dashti, an Iranian author and a committed Muslim, commented that the errors in the Koran were so many that the grammatical rules had to be altered in order to fit the claim that the Koran was flawless. He gives numerous examples of these in his book, *Twenty-Three Years: The Life of the Prophet Mohammed.* (The only precaution he took before publishing this book was to direct that it be published posthumously.)

A further problem facing the early compilers of the Koran was the number of variant readings of some of the important texts. Now, in recent times, scholars have begun to look at the Koran and have raised some very serious questions regarding its origin and compilation. This has sent many Islamic scholars scrambling for a response.[5]

What one does need to grant is that the poetry and the style are beautiful. The postmodern, visually controlled mind has much to learn about the place of beauty in speech. But the question before us is whether this book can be considered to be the word of God. Also, considering that Islam claims Mohammed to be a prophet to the world, the "miracle" is limited to one language, a significant portion of which is considered incomprehensible, even to those who know the language. In other words, to truly see the miracle, one has not only to speak Arabic, but also to be highly sophisticated in it. Rather narrow and highly restrictive is a claim such as that.

As for truth and the Hindus, the terrain gets very rocky. Gandhi, for example, said, "God is truth and truth is God."[6] But what does that mean? It does not answer the more fundamental question of whether the existence of God is true or false. Shankara, one of the principal exponents of Hinduism, evaded that question by saying that while a person *may* worship God, it is only an inferior way of expressing truth. Ultimately, the worshiper moves to the supreme truth that he is identical with God. The bottom line is that the Hindus point to their scriptures as truth. Here, the challenge is very complex.

The Hindu scriptures actually fall into two broad categories—the Smriti and the Sruti. *Smriti* means, "That which is remembered." The authors are many and the assertions they make are diametrically different. In this corpus lie the speculations of Indian sages, ranging from the profound to the utterly bizarre, by their own admission. *Sruti*, on the other hand, means, "That which was revealed." This is the eternally true revelation of the devout Hindu.

If this revelation is eternally true, then the religion cannot claim that all ways are true for the simple reason that some religions deny the eternal veracity of the Vedas. Muslims, Buddhists, and Christians would deny such a claim. As a matter of fact, even some Hindu scholars would deny that claim. Either their denial is true, or the claim of the Hindu is true.

But, there is a deeper question. If "that which was revealed" is the eternal authority, then the logical question for pantheism, which claims that all is one, is, Who is doing the revealing? To even attempt to answer this would take a book by itself. Some words from Sri Ramakrishna will reveal the problem.

> God alone is, and it is He who has become this universe. . . . "As the snake I bite, as the healer I cure." God is the ignorant man and God is the enlightened man. God as the ignorant man remains deluded. Again, He as the guru gives enlightenment to God in the ignorant.[7]

We see the mind-boggling implications of such a view of God and revelation. If all that exists is God, then all that we know is either God in ignorance or God in enlightenment. The question arises, then, that when Buddha rejected the Vedas, was he God in ignorance or God in enlightenment? When Mohammed posited monotheism and the way of submission to Allah, was he God in ignorance or God in enlightenment? So run the sequence of questions when all that exists is God. The revealer and the receptor are the same, only in different stages of truth.

By dramatic contrast, the Christian view of revelation is given to us in the Scriptures. The claim of the writers is set forth clearly:

> Above all, you must understand that no prophecy of Scripture came about by the prophet's own interpretation. For prophecy never had its origin in the will of man, but men spoke from God as they were carried along by the Holy Spirit. (2 Pet. 1:20–21)

The Bible also says that "in the past God spoke to our forefathers through the prophets at many times and in various ways, but in these last days he has spoken to us by his Son" (Heb. 1:1–2).

What, then, is the difference? Is it only one of a claim? No. First of all, in contrast to the Koran, the Bible was written not by one author, but by several human authors. The Bible was written over a fifteen-hundred-year span, by writers from various backgrounds, times, and learning, who, under God's inspiration, wrote down the revelation. Over that vast span of time, their message is one—they point to the birth, the death, and the resurrection of God's Son, Jesus Christ. When you think about it, that is an incredible confluence of thought over nearly two millennia. The spread itself defies natural explanation. Long before all converged in the person of Jesus Christ, His coming was envisioned, foreshadowed, and described in detail. After His death, the written Scriptures spoke of the life so dramatically born, lived, crucified, and risen. In other words, God has spoken and given to us His Word. And the climax of that Word is the person of Jesus Christ. The written Word is complete. He is perfect. He reminded us that the Scriptures cannot be broken—His Word never falters.

Further, in the fulfillment of the prophecy, as He stood silent, He showed another aspect of scriptural authority. The Bible is not merely a self-referencing book, but a book in which history, geography, and the miraculous content of prophecy and other acts were subject to the principle of verification. Some of those supernatural elements we have already seen in the other chapters, claimed and defended.

Thus, when Jesus stood before His accusers in silence, He had already prophesied in His Word centuries before that He would be silent before them. They knew the Scriptures and were even spoken of in them, but they suppressed the truth to justify their unrighteous lives. Both attitudes converged in fulfillment. They who marveled at His silence lost the wonder of what He had said. By His words and His silence, and by their words and their deeds, we see that the trial was exactly as God's Word stated it would be. We see in that His regard for His Word and our disregard for it.

Are we willing yet to listen and to see ourselves portrayed in the Scriptures? In a world of noise, the silence of God can be terrifying. Martin Luther once cried out, "Bless us, Lord! Yea, even curse us. But please be not silent!" Thanks be to God, He is not silent toward us. That is why the apostle Paul said to young Timothy:

> But as for you, continue in what you have learned . . . and how from infancy you have known the holy Scriptures, which are able to make you wise for salvation through faith in Christ Jesus. All Scripture is God-breathed and is useful for

teaching, rebuking, correcting and training in righteousness, so that the man of God may be thoroughly equipped for every good work. (2 Tim. 3:14–17)

One more thing needs to be said. Just before Sir Thomas More went to his death, his daughter, Margaret, asked him why he couldn't just give verbal consent and mutter words of support to the king without having to really mean them. She justified that life-saving ploy by saying, "You are the one who told me that it is the thoughts that one looks at and not the words. Just say it. Don't mean it." More's response to her is brilliant.

It's a poor argument, Meg. When a man takes an oath, he's holding his own self in his own hands. Like water [he cups hands], and if he opens his fingers, then— he needn't hope to find himself again. Some men aren't capable of this, but I'd loathe to think your father one of them.[8]

The makeshift court and More's own family reasoned with him that he could say something without meaning it. More reminded them that the word of a person was only as good as he is. One's word was one's life.

This is an enormous truth. That is why Jesus did not fear His accusers. He was committed by His Word. He, above all, lived a life where the word and life were identical. Of no other life can this be said. Either there was a breakdown within one's word, or there was a breakdown between the life and the word. Jesus, by honoring His Word, offered them and us His life. He did not merely die for justice. He died in prophetic fulfillment, demonstrating that you cannot kill the truth. Therefore, in a real sense, they could not destroy Him either.

I once saw a poster on the wall in the office of a school principal. It simply said, "If you cannot understand me in my speech, how can you understand me in my silence?"

The world will try to interpret truth by its wits. The Christian interprets truth by His Word—and by His silence.

Chapter Seven

IS THERE A GARDENER?

"WHY ARE YOU CRYING? WHO IS IT YOU ARE LOOKING FOR?"

That was the question asked of Mary when she went to the garden where the body of Jesus had been laid in a tomb. During the few short years that the disciples had with Jesus, their conversations had abounded with questions. There is, therefore, a tender note of indictment when this question is asked of *them*. This actually has overtones of a question He had asked them on more than one occasion. To His earliest followers, He had asked, "What do you want?" He had asked the same of the disciples of John the Baptizer—"What did you go out to see?" One has to presume that He repeatedly stopped them to ask of themselves what it was that they wanted God to be in order to merit their approval.

During their years with Him, their inability to grasp so much of what He said wins both our sympathy and our bewilderment. Indeed, they were with One who was like no other, and therefore, their tentative posture every step of the way is understandable. But how much more specific did He have to be before they were clear as to who He was?

The trail to this question is actually one that spans the breadth of human existence and goes back across millennia to another setting, when the first man and woman were placed in a garden and the questions of life and death began. In brief, the story of Jesus of Nazareth could be succinctly told around the setting of four gardens. I have selected this as the framework in which I want to present some of the most convincing evidence of the uniqueness of Jesus Christ in history and in the religions of the world.

HIDING TO SEEK

Many years ago, philosophers Anthony Flew and John Wisdom drafted a parable, posing the question of God's existence in the following way:

Once upon a time two explorers came upon a clearing in the jungle. In the clearing growing side by side were many flowers and many weeds. One of the explorers exclaimed, "Some gardener must tend this plot!" So they pitched their tents and set a watch.

But though they waited several days no gardener was seen.

"Perhaps he is an invisible gardener!" they thought. So they set up a barbed-wire fence and connected it to electricity. They even patrolled the garden with bloodhounds, for they remembered that H. G. Wells's "Invisible Man" could be both smelt and touched though he could not be seen. But no sounds ever suggested that someone had received an electric shock. No movements of the wire ever betrayed an invisible climber. The bloodhounds never alerted them to the presence of any other in the garden than themselves. Yet, still the believer between them was convinced that there was indeed a gardener.

"There must be a gardener, invisible, intangible, insensible to electric shocks, a gardener who has no scent and makes no sound, a gardener who comes secretly to look after the garden which he loves."

At last the skeptical explorer despaired, "But what remains of your original assertion? Just how does what you call an invisible, intangible, eternally elusive gardener differ from an imaginary gardener or even from no gardener at all?"[1]

The point of the parable is clear. How many times have we ourselves asked that we might see God, just to be assured that He is actually there? But with all of our waiting and watching, like the explorers looking for the gardener, we do not see Him, yet still we contend that He is there. The atheist looks pleadingly and says, "Show me God." Our answers seem evasive because we do not have any visible body to point to. Flew and Wisdom ask the question of us: What is the difference between an invisible, elusive gardener and no gardener at all? It is a question well taken.

Philosopher John Frame responded with a brilliant counterpoint. This is his parable.

Once upon a time, two explorers came upon a clearing in the jungle. A man was there, pulling weeds, applying fertilizer, and trimming branches. The man turned to the explorers and introduced himself as the royal gardener. One explorer shook his hand and exchanged pleasantries. The other ignored the gardener and turned away.

"There can be no gardener in this part of the jungle," he said. "This must be some trick. Someone is trying to discredit our secret findings."

They pitched camp. And every day the gardener arrived to tend the garden. Soon it was bursting with perfectly arranged blooms. But the skeptical explorer insisted, "He's only doing it because we are here—to fool us into thinking that this is a royal garden."

One day the gardener took them to the royal palace and introduced the explorers to a score of officials who verified the gardener's status. Then the skeptic tried a last resort, "Our senses are deceiving us. There is no gardener, no blooms, no palace, and no officials. It's all a hoax!"

Finally the believing explorer despaired, "But what remains of your original assertion? Just how does this mirage differ from a real gardener?"[2]

John Frame's point is equally well taken. There is so much intelligibility and specified complexity in this world that it seems willful and prejudiced to try to explain it away with no intelligence behind it. Can morality, personality, and reality be reasonably explained without a personal, moral first cause? How does one explain some of the features of a garden apart from there being a gardener? What kind of proof for a gardener will suffice anyway? What if the gardener did come and was seen and desires that our trust in his work not be dependent on only a direct sighting of him, because the essence of our relationship is not the constancy of sight and intervention, but the steadfastness of trust and sufficiency?

Between the taunt brought by Flew and Wisdom in their parable and the answer given by Frame in his parable, where are we left? Is the evidence for the existence of God merely a matter of perspective? Can each side just deride the other and leave it at that? Interestingly enough, the last question the disciples faced when they went looking for Jesus addresses the questions raised by these very parables. Is there a gardener in this combination of flowers and weeds that we call Planet Earth?

It is a bit of a winding path to follow. But when we get to the end, the reason for this journey might open up new vistas. The goal will be to see whether or not He has spoken to us and how Christ has revealed God to us.

IT BEGAN IN A GARDEN

The biblical narrative opens with the words "In the beginning." The focus moves quickly to the world God created, the crowning point of which was the creation of man and woman. The context shows a world of relationship, purpose, and beauty, with natural law set in place and stewardship over creation entrusted to human beings.

Tragically, naturalism (in which all reality is explained in natural terms) and theism have collided in these opening verses of the Bible. Instead of understanding the intention and the context of those to whom the revelation was given, the naturalist mocks the Bible's description of God's act of creation as bereft of scientific sophistication. On the other extreme is the theist who tries to make the record of creation look like a cosmologist's dissertation and then struggles to defend it.

No portion of Scripture ever claims to be a piece of scientifically technical material, intended to satisfy a technician's mind. I have repeatedly heard popular iconoclasts ridicule the ancient belief that the earth was flat and the belief that the world was created in 4004 B.C., declaring these assertions to be taught in the Bible. They never pause to prove their point by showing you where they have read that in the Bible.

Since that historic and histrionic Scopes trial in 1925, any discussion between a theist and an atheist on the question of origins is treated as if only a fool would now hold that a supernatural origin to this world is plausible. As frequently as that landmark trial is dragged into the conversation, castigating the Christian view of origins, I have discovered that most who talk about it have never even read the script and the context surrounding the trial. (They have seen the movie, to be sure.)

In this closing chapter, it is not my intention to reopen that conflict because there are already superb works that bring this debate into modern-day dialogue. But that snub at the hands of capable challengers still hangs over us like a pall. I return to it for a brief moment only to point out the fallacy and prejudice embraced then and espoused even now. If the tables were turned and the method used then against the theist were used against the naturalist, the derision could be just as loud.

A Page from the Past

What was that fallacy? Let us start with the backdrop, which itself was a travesty. The trial took place in Dayton, Tennessee, in 1925. The emotions ran deep, as the media harnessed an event and tailored it to full entertainment value. Predictably, the larger points were missed. There were so many issues that were woven through the proceedings that one has to wonder whether the setting, the arguments, or the process had anything to do with the specifics of the case. If today one were to analyze the questioning by Clarence Darrow of William Jennings Bryan, it would be readily seen that Darrow's answers to an equally adept challenge would have been at least as unconvincing. His whole scheme was to persuade Bryan to take the stand in defense of the miraculous and then to destroy him. Bryan thought he was up to it, and for him, it was the equivalent of getting O. J. Simpson to try on the glove. The supernatural elements of the Scripture as caricatured by Darrow did not fit the "scientific" framework, and Bryan looked bedraggled and defeated.

But was that really the way to determine whether the Bible could be trusted as a document on origins? Herein is the fallacy. Can particulars of a world-view be defended without first defending the world-view itself? It defies logic that something so methodologically tendentious could be taken as compelling proof. Any brilliant lawyer can tell you that in most trials, when only selected facts are permitted into the courtroom, any adept wordsmith can construct a farce. The added component of the media only compounds the sham.

Think of this. One of the questions for which Mr. Darrow demanded an answer of William Jennings Bryan was where Cain got his wife. That could be a fair question if it were permitted that the Bible could first be defended in its intent and content, and if the assertion were also made that it contained every detail of how human reproduction began. But none of that was even given possibility. So let us reverse the questioning and challenge the naturalist to, in effect, answer the same question. How did the first *Homo sapiens* get "his" or "her" partner? Predictably, our entire values orientation is defined on answers to this. Could Mr. Darrow have sounded very persuasive here?

How did human sexuality and marriage emerge in the evolutionary scheme of things? I would like to have asked Mr. Darrow to explain how the "Big Bang" came to confer on sexuality the enormous combination of intimacy, pleasure, consummation, conception, gestation, nurture, and supererogatory expressions of care and love. All this came from the explosion of a singularity? In no other discipline would so much information density be swallowed up under the nomenclature of chance. In case Mr. Darrow was not forthcoming with an answer, I could help him even with the most modern research.

William Hamilton of Oxford has offered one theory (this is serious, by the way): "Sex is for combating parasites." You see, in warm and rich climates where microscopic parasites threaten the stable health of their hosts, the hosts mess up the attacking power of these foes through sex and procreation. That is the reason sex came to be: to stay ahead of the game![3]

My! How different prescriptions look today to ancient cures. Imagine what the late-night comedians could do with this material. The laughter could be even more hilarious than the derision afforded to Bryan.

The shredding of fine points bereft of a studied understanding of the base of truth on which it all stands is an illicit process in which anything can be made to look absolutely idiotic. You do not form a conclusion on the presence of a gardener by studying only one bush. There is much more.

And here we see in small print what really should be the larger point. A glance at the sidebars of the trial actually betrays where the real prejudice lay, as it does to this day. On the third day of the trial, the judge asked a minister present to open in prayer. The controversy engendered was almost a circus in itself. But in spite of Clarence Darrow's strong objection, the judge allowed the prayer to proceed. Darrow's team of attorneys then rounded up a group of ministers to sign a petition objecting to the prayer on the grounds that their particular theological persuasion was not represented in it. That objection was denied by the judge. Finally, they submitted another petition signed by two Unitarian ministers, one Congregationalist minister, and one rabbi. It stated that they believed that God had shown Himself as much in the wonders of the world as He had in the written Word, and hence, a prayer that did not reflect that was abhorrent to them.

One can only shake one's head in disbelief. How ironic that "the wonders of the world" were placed on equal footing with God's spoken Word, while all along the very case being argued was whether these wonders required natural or supernatural explanation. You see, the real issue was not the explicability of the material world. The real issue was whether God had spoken through language as well as through nature.

Eden surfaced again—"Did God really say that?" Is there only a garden to look at, or is there also a voice with which the gardener speaks?

In the same manner as that small-town trial, we bring this prejudice to Genesis and think that we are capable of deciding whether God acted in six days or through fifteen billion years. That was not the intention at all. The four major thoughts of the Genesis text have been lost in the volume of extraneous debate. The principal thrust in the opening pages of Genesis is that God is the Creator and that He is both personal and eternal—He is a living, communicating God. The second is that the world did not come by accident, but was designed with humanity in mind—man is an intelligent, spiritual being. The third thrust is that life could not be lived out alone but through companionship—man is a relational, dependent being. The fourth aspect is that man was fashioned as a moral entity with the privilege of self-determination—man is an accountable, rational being.

Three significant relationships entail: that of man toward God—the sanctity of worship; that of man toward his spouse and fellow human beings—

the sanctity of relationship; and that of man toward the created order—the sanctity of stewardship. Upon and from the first flow the other two.

If this order is contrasted with that of the naturalist, the following pattern emerges. The impersonal universe brought itself into being and just happened to strike upon the conditions in which life could arise—the elimination of any ultimate purpose. Somehow over time, in order to thwart disease and destruction and to survive, procreation brought multiplication—the materiality and amorality of sex. Codes were developed that were mutually beneficial—the cultural and relative nature of morality.

Every assertion in that paradigm flies in the face of reason and intuition. It is scientifically and existentially incoherent. Take just the first. Bare nothing has never been known to produce something. Can one scientifically explain how a state of absolute nothingness can bring about intelligent processes and results? However one wants to disagree on the processes, the fact is that this is an ontologically haunted universe. By that, I mean that the ultimate cause of our being and our very mode of thinking demand that what we are and how we came to be cannot just be dismissed as "it happened." There is intelligibility running through our veins, and from that we cannot run.

Every deduction of the naturalist can be readily countered, from our coming into being to the relationships we experience with others, to the moral imperatives in our lives. That is why, may I add, millions, indeed billions, in this world will never shrug off the supernatural no matter how high the naturalist raises his volume. Not because those billions are fools, but because plain intuitive certainty tells them that something with such spiritual and physical complexity just cannot come from nothing.

You see, in the Genesis account, the question is not whether the garden was by design or by accident. That was the most reasonable recognition. Rather, doubt was planted as to whether or not God had spoken and given the ground rules for life. The answer from the naturalist is a thunderous "No!" To accept that God has spoken is to surrender the first principles of naturalism. So the real debate is distracted by mockery and by name-calling. The difference between name-calling and calling one by name is world-views apart. I will explain this when the argument is unfolded. But at the outset, we see that the difference between a silent world and one in which God has spoken is the dramatic line of division between the theist and the naturalist.

A VOLUME OF SILENCE

Some time ago, I had to undergo an examination using magnetic resonance imaging to diagnose a disc herniation in my lower back. This was one of those experiences in which the examination seemed to be at least as distressing—if not more so—than the problem itself. I was laid on a movable table and slid into a narrow tunnel where the door was shut on me. The confines were so small and the darkness so grim that I am convinced that whoever designed it must have received his or her inspiration from studying Egyptian sarcophagi. Humor aside, it was a terrifying experience, especially for one who is claustrophobic, as I am. Moments after the door was shut, I was in a pitch-black, silent world. Long, fearsome seconds ticked away, and then at last the technician's voice crackled through an electronic speaker in the capsule, "Before I begin, do you have any questions?" he asked. Did I ever have questions! I nervously blurted back, "Sir! Will you be there the whole time that I am in here?" He answered, "I promise you, Mr. Zacharias, that I will be here through the entire length of the procedure."

Just recounting the incident sends a shiver through me. I want you to know that even a total stranger's voice was of immense comfort to me in this closed box that had me in its clasp. As I lay there, a horrifying thought suddenly came upon me. In the naturalistic scheme, humanity has been tossed into this closed system called the universe, and we are hurtling through space, with no voice out there to speak to us. There is nobody to ask us if we have any questions, and nobody to tell us that he is there for us. As one comedian put it, "We are in this together, alone." We are on our own. That is the world Darrow was, in effect, arguing for. And it is a world the Bible soundly rejects. God is, and God has spoken.

You see, if there is no voice from without, we are the cause and the keepers of the garden. All relationships may be legitimately redefined. We speak to ourselves. We define ourselves. We regulate ourselves. Free society mocks any self-regulating body, yet when it comes down to living in a community, that is precisely what we do. Notice the number of laws the free world must enact in order to keep us from destroying this garden because there is no gardener but us. The naturalist is merely looking for himself. There is no one to speak to us but ourselves.

God, by contrast, hung it all on one law—to love the Lord your God with all your heart and soul and mind, and to love your neighbor as yourself. That is not enscripted in the planets; it is written for us in His Word. By His grace, He has placed this law into our hearts. When we toss it out of our hearts, questioning if He has indeed spoken, innumerable laws must be written in the place of God's law, and countless agencies must be formed to enforce those laws.

There is yet a further point of inference. From this silent, lonely world within, there logically followed a disintegration of those very relationships that Genesis revealed as being sacred. Genesis did not tell us how Cain got his wife because in the world of which God is the Creator, that is a secondary concern. In fact, when God spoke to Adam and Eve of the priority of husband and wife over father and mother, there were not even fathers and mothers at that time. Genesis did tell us that a man and a wife were in a loving, binding relationship, blessed by God, and progenitors of the human race through the establishment of the home. The home and the family were God's idea, not ours. Cain rejected that, murdered his brother, and broke the hearts of his parents—and the family was ruptured. The garden became a jungle of fear and death.

Those same implications are with us today, as the following story illustrates. Some years ago, Edmund Gosse wrote a very powerful book entitled *Father and Son.* It is the gripping and true account of a son's struggle between the faith of his father and his own growing doubts of God's existence. His father was a marine biologist while he, the son, was a lecturer in English literature who later became the librarian at the British House of Lords. In the book he traced his journey into skepticism to the day when he finally told his father that he was through with God and could no longer bring himself to believe in His existence.

The father wrote back in the most heart-wrenching terms. Toward the end of the book, Gosse quotes that letter in its entirety, and says, "It buried itself like an arrow within my heart." Here are some excerpts from his father's letter.

My dear son,

When your mother died, she not only tenderly committed you to God, but left you as a solemn charge to me, to bring you up in the nurture and admonition of the Lord. That responsibility I have sought to keep before me. . . . Before your childhood passed, there seemed God's manifest blessing on your care; for you seemed truly converted to Him. . . . All this filled my heart with thankfulness and joy. . . .

[But] when you came to us in the summer, the heavy blow fell upon me; and I discovered how very far you had departed from God. It was not that you had yielded to the strong tide of youthful blood . . . it was that which had already worked in your mind . . . sapping the very foundations of faith. Nothing seemed left to which I could appeal. We had, I found, no common ground. The Holy Scriptures had no longer any authority. . . . Any oracle of God that pressed you, you could easily explain away; even the very character of God you weighed in your balance of reason and fashioned it accordingly. You were thus sailing down the rapid tide towards eternity without a single authoritative guide (having cast your chart overboard), except what you might fashion and forge on your own anvil. . . .

It is with pain, not in anger that I [write] . . . hoping that you may be induced to review the whole course, of which this is only a stage, before God. If this grace were granted to you, oh! How joyfully should I bury all the past, and again have sweet and tender fellowship with my beloved son, as of old.[4]

So ended the letter. Edmund made his response, telling the reader that he had a choice, either "to retain his intelligence and reject God" or "to reject his intelligence and submit to God." This is how he closed his book, speaking in the third person:

And thus desperately challenged, the young man's conscience threw off once and for all the yoke of his "dedication," and as respectfully as he could, without parade or remonstrance, he took a human being's privilege to fashion his inner life for himself.[5]

Their relationship was permanently severed. How did it all come about? Darwin's *Origin of Species* fell into the hands of young Gosse, and that was the beginning. The more he thought of it and wrestled with it, he concluded that if need be, he was willing to forfeit everything—including fellowship with God and with his family. If there was no home for the heart in any ultimate sense, why should there be one in any temporal sense? With Darwin's volume in hand, Edmund forged a purpose that had no compass but one of his own making.

This true story serves as a real but reflective throwback to what happened in the garden as God created it. The heart of the question was raised: Has God really spoken? When Adam and Eve questioned the authority of God, the allurement placed before them was that they could become as God, defining good and evil. What the tempter did not tell them was that good and evil as defined by God are rooted in His character, and there is nothing contradictory in God. Good and evil as defined by fallen humanity are born out of a spirit of rebellion that results in the disintegration of life. Can any reasonable person not see the difference as it has been played out in human history?

We live amid the devastation of the three sanctities: worship, relationship, and stewardship. Charles Darwin himself feared that the philosophical ramifications of natural selection had dire entailments. "Nature red in tooth and claw" was not just a poet's description, but the reality of a rebellion from a transcendent moral law. The mockery and ridicule in the Scopes trial was not the mockery of an intellectual over a lunatic. It was the mockery of the voice of man over the voice of God.

In the first garden, God spoke, and humanity denied that He had. Humanism was born, and man became the source of meaning.

ROCKS AND HUNGER

Now we come to the second garden, and here a strange twist is added. The question in this setting was not so much whether God had, in fact, spoken, but whether what He said could be contoured into something other than what He meant. The setting was ideal for distortion because it was not so much a garden as it was a desert. Gardens can seduce one by the beauty of the surroundings, delighting in the aesthetic while denouncing the moral. By contrast, deserts can generate mirages so that what is actually unreal and imaginary looks real. In the first, the deception is that of the will; in the second, the disorientation is that of the mind. The very paradigm is shifted, and truth is at the mercy of the imagination.

Jesus was hungry and physically weak, and the tempter stormed Him with a series of taunts. One of those gibes thrown was, "Jump, and see if Your Father will honor His word." Every temptation was fused with the same challenge: "Why don't You do this Your own way and prove Your autonomy?"

What, then, is the twist? In Eden, the question was one of the text: Did God actually speak? Here, it is one of context: Change the meaning of the text, and you play God. While in the first setting humanism was born, in the second, religion without truth was born—a form of polytheism, many gods, or pantheism, in which individuality is exalted to divinity. The irony here is that though Jesus was divine, He could not lay claim to His power without forfeiting His mission.

The inability to think in context is so manifest in the moral conflicts that we live with today. Every major moral battle we fight is either because we deny the text or because we justify the contrary by appealing to a different context. By the change of a word or by justification of some other kind, nothing is essentially good or evil anymore.

Something far-reaching comes to birth as a result. Common sense tells us that we cannot live without a moral law. But how does one generate a moral law if God has not spoken? The only answer is to arrange a morality of one's own design that, though mystical and transcendent, is attainable by one's own efforts. This way we appeal to our spiritual bent and at the same time incorporate our self at the center. If we can be good without God but retain a religiosity, we win both the secular and the sacred.

The New Age philosophies came in order to satisfy this demand. What better way to apply an economic theory of supply and demand than to manufacture a religion that is in limitless supply and can be tailored to fit one's personal demand? A personalized religion with an impersonal God—that's what it is. This kind of religion by its nature has an immense capacity to reflect the pragmatic, a chameleon's dream. In the desert, the temptation was not to invent a naturalistic explanation as much as it was to reinterpret the revelation by massaging the context.

No religions have done more to prove the reality of this temptation than Hinduism and Buddhism. With repeated effort, noted scholars and practitioners have tried to shade the truths of Christianity and make them resemble their own world-views. Verses such as, "The kingdom of God is in you," or "I and My Father are One" are used to sustain pantheism. Some of the most renowned Hindu philosophers have strained to make this point and tell us there is no difference. Any reading of the context in which these statements in Scripture were made shows clearly the illicit use of the texts by those who seek to distort them.

This reasoning is in violation of both logic and theism. What begins with a subtle departure from the truth by the allurement of self-deification ultimately results in the deification of everyone and everything. Such a world would be destroyed by powers of conflict because every power would claim autonomy. That is why Hinduism's epics are full of war and killing as an integral part of being gods and goddesses. Animal features emerge on the divine, the stories behind them leaving one utterly puzzled. And into the mix of polytheism and pantheism, other divinities are added—rivers, wind, and fire. The world of god-making had begun.

The Christian Scriptures are dramatically different. When God sent the plagues upon Egypt in the Old Testament, they were designed to show that He alone was supreme over the objects that they had deified (rivers, planets, creatures, magic, and so on) and that there was no other like Him. Nature, humanity, and every other entity or quantity is distinct from God. We cannot try to eliminate that distinction with impunity. From pantheism to the worship of nature, the temptation of the desert is still with us today, to have religion without God.

Rejecting the text of God in the first garden paved the way for humanism, and rejecting His context in the second led to polytheism or pantheism—many gods or self-deification.

THE GARDEN OF PAIN

The third garden is the point on which I wish to truly focus because, by any standard of measurement, here the Christian faith offers an answer for which no other system even pretends to find a substitute.

Having withstood the test in which He was challenged to go His own way, in this garden Jesus now kneels at the most desolate moment of His mission. It was to accomplish this mission that He resisted the urge to invoke the supernatural as an easy way out.

All the Gospel writers place Him at Gethsemane when the betrayal by Judas took place. Matthew in particular gives us an extensive look at the anguish of Jesus in those moments preceding His arrest. That garden has become synonymous with loneliness, sorrow, pain, and death. The events that took place during those hours had to be a source of great embarrassment to the disciples when they were happening and an even greater humiliation when they reported it after the fact. They do not flatter themselves here, and the reason they do not is because they had never expected to see Him or themselves in this time of horror. This was not what they had "come to see." How could the Son of God be in such anguish and in the throes of death? Was not death itself the greatest enemy to be conquered? How could it conquer the Author of life?

Once they understood the purpose and the means of His death, it became the riveting truth of the gospel they preached with unshakable conviction. The apostle Paul said, "We preach Christ crucified . . . Christ the power of God and the wisdom of God" (1 Cor. 1:23–24). He went on to add, "I resolved to know nothing while I was with you except Jesus Christ and him crucified" (1 Cor. 2:2).

What is the cross all about? How can that which the Greeks considered foolishness and over which the Jews stumbled (see 1 Cor. 1:21) be described as the power of God? To this day, it does not sound like a work of power to any kingdom builder. Pascal once referred to humanity as the glory and the shame of the universe. In the cross, we see why that is an appropriate description.

COMING CLOSE TO THE CROSS

Theologian Martin Hengel has written an extraordinary book called *Crucifixion: The Ancient World and the Folly of the Cross*. Hengel takes the reader through the grim and historic details of all that crucifixion meant and implied, and in particular, the crucifixion of Jesus. In his summary at the end he makes several points. I will present just a few of them.

> Crucifixion was a political and military punishment, and while the Persians and Carthaginians inflicted it upon high officials, the Romans used it on the lower classes—slaves, violent criminals, and unruly elements in society.
>
> Crucifying an individual satisfied principally a lust for revenge and brought great sadistic pleasure. It was the triumph of the state.
>
> By displaying the victim naked, at a prominent place, crucifixion represented the uttermost of humiliation.
>
> Often, the victim was never buried, so that wild beasts could feed on the carcass.[6]

Think about it. If death in itself is a "defeat," how much more a death in which politics, revenge, and power inflict their mark on the crucified one. These are institutions and attitudes with which we measure influence. To the disciples, principally Jewish, this punishment signified the loss of everything. Anger, power, pride, and cruelty were victorious over the One who claimed to be God.

Millennia later, we see the symbol of the cross on necklaces and on church steeples so often that we have no concept of what it meant and accomplished. In fact, if it were truly expounded upon, we would take offense at the preacher. Hengel helps us in his concluding remarks:

> It is impossible to dissociate talk of the atoning death of Jesus or the blood of Jesus from this "word of the cross." The spearhead cannot be broken off the spear. Rather, the complex of the death of Jesus is . . . that . . . Jesus did not die a gentle death like Socrates, with his cup of hemlock, much less passing on "old and

full of years" like the patriarchs of the Old Testament. Rather, he died like a slave or a common criminal, in torment, on the tree of shame. . . . Jesus did not die just any death; he was "given up for us all" on the cross, in a cruel and a contemptible way. Reflection on the harsh reality of crucifixion in antiquity may help us overcome the acute loss of reality which is to be found so often in present theology and preaching.[7]

I might add, "The acute loss of reality which is to be found so often today, both in preaching and in hearing." We do not seem to have the capacity to reflectively hear anymore, even if it were preached.

The first and foremost reality is that suffering and death are not only enemies of life, but a means of reminding us of life's twin realities, love and hate. Here, the love and hate did not just happen. The paths were chosen. Those who hurt Him hated Him. Those who hated Him, He loved. Those who killed Him wanted to be rid of Him. By allowing Himself to be killed, He made it possible for them to live. The crucifixion of Jesus was the embodied expression of rebellion against God. His desolation was a profound attempt to break apart the very being of God, in the Holy Trinity.

But here is the point. He did not die as a martyr for a cause, as others have done; nor was He just nonviolent so that the enemy would surrender through public outcry, as still others have done. He did not even die because He was willing to pay the price that someone else would live. *He came to lay down His life so that the very ones who killed Him, who represented all of us, could be forgiven because of the price that He paid in the hell of a world that does not recognize His voice.* Those who had rejected the text and manipulated the context of His Word saw and heard what God incarnate disclosed of reality. Every feeling they experienced, every state of mind, every utterance was the opposite of what Jesus felt, did, and said. His counterperspective stands in brilliant and sharp contrast, even as He invited them on the basis of that death to come to Him for forgiveness, because He longed to reach out to them.

In *Crime and Punishment,* Dostoevsky writes these lines of God's invitation:

Then Christ will say to us, "Come you as well, Come drunkards, come weaklings, come forth ye children of shame. . . ." And the wise men and those of understanding will say: "O Lord, why do you receive these men?" And he will say, "This is why I receive them, O ye of understanding, that not one of them believed himself to be worthy of this." And he will hold out his hands to us and we shall fall down before him . . . and we shall weep . . . and we shall understand all things! . . . Lord, thy kingdom come.[8]

Henry Nouwen, whose short life was characterized by a deep commitment to Jesus Christ, tells of a very moving personal experience. Nouwen, as some might not know, was a distinguished scholar, having taught at the University of Notre Dame and at Harvard University. He gave it all up to work with the mentally retarded at a center in Toronto. In his book *The Return of the Prodigal Son* he brings to life one of Rembrandt's paintings.

He had been profoundly affected by Rembrandt's depiction of the prodigal son returning to the waiting father, in whose arms he was clasped. Nouwen journeyed to see the original painting and admitted to being apprehensive, lest the work be less than what his imagination suggested. This is how he words the impact, after sitting in front of the painting for four hours:

And so there I was; facing the painting that had been on my mind and in my heart for nearly three years. I was stunned by its majestic beauty. Its size, larger than life; its abundant reds, browns, and yellows; its shadowy recess and bright foreground, but most of all the light-enveloped embrace of father and son surrounded by four mysterious bystanders, all of this gripped me with an intensity far beyond my anticipation. There had been moments in which I had wondered whether the real painting might disappoint me. The opposite was true. Its grandeur and splendor made everything recede into the background and held me completely captivated.

Rembrandt's embrace remained imprinted on my soul far more profoundly than any temporary expression of emotional support. It has brought me into touch with something within me that lies far beyond the ups and downs of life, something that represents the ongoing yearning of the human spirit, the yearning for a final return, an unambiguous sense of safety, a lasting home.[9]

Those closing lines strike deep into my own soul—"An unambiguous sense of safety, a lasting home." I have lived half of my life out of a suitcase, sometimes seeing this world more from thirty-seven thousand feet in the air rather than on terra firma. I have to check and recheck where I have left my passport and wallet and all the other things that form the luggage of life on the road. I lock my suitcases each time I leave the hotel room and twirl the combination lock. There are visas from places near and far stamped in my passport. Border officers or guards have carried out their routines dozens of times in my life. I walk ever conscious of being on foreign soil, with an over-the-shoulder awareness. Oh! for an unambiguous sense of safety in a lasting home. It is the reality of the cross cut deeply into my soul that brings comfort of a final home that awaits me. I can identify with the songwriter who wrote,

> O Love that wilt not let me go,
> I rest my weary soul in Thee;
> I give Thee back the life I owe,
> That in Thine ocean depths its flow
> May richer fuller be.
>
> O Cross that liftest up my head,
> I dare not ask to fly from Thee;
> I lay in dust life's glory dead,
> And from the ground there blossoms red
> Life that shall endless be.[10]

When the missionary John Paton arrived in the New Hebrides in the mid-1800s, he began translation on the New Testament. First, he had to reduce their language to writing. He worked with his young helper to come up with the vocabulary. He did not know how to illustrate the word *believe*. Finally, when he leaned completely on a chair in such a way that his whole weight was on it, the concept of trust emerged. John 3:16 now reads in their Bible, "For God so loved the world, that He gave His one and only Son, that whoever throws his whole weight on Him, will not perish but have eternal life."

Such is the procurement of the cross. A form of Christianity that goes by that name but loses sight of the cross is not Christian. A "religious" person that thinks nature and the cross portend no difference understands neither. His cross is the hill from which our gardens are addressed. His was a crown of thorns. His voice rings above the sounds of hate and torture and death, "Father forgive them, for they know not what they do."

This carries us beyond the text and the context to the contest—whose way? God's way or ours? The Garden of Gethsemane pointed Jesus to the cross.

THE LAST GARDEN

From the Garden of Gethsemane, which preceded the Cross of Calvary, we move now to the final garden. After Jesus was crucified, two men came and asked Pilate for permission to take His body down from the cross and entomb Him. They were men who, when Jesus was alive, were afraid to follow Him openly. One was Joseph of Arimathea, whom the Bible describes as a secret follower. The other was a teacher who had earlier come to Jesus at night so that he would not be seen in His company. His name was Nicodemus.

Nicodemus and Joseph brought a sack of myrrh and aloes and, along with spices and strips of cloth, they wrapped Jesus' body in keeping with Jewish custom. But His enemies were nervous. They went to Pilate and asked to have a guard placed around the tomb because they feared the body would be stolen by His disciples who would then claim that He had risen from the dead, just as He had declared He would.

This I find startling. Utterly startling! Jesus' enemies evidently knew what Jesus meant better than His own followers did. The disciples were hiding in fear of being arrested and sharing in Jesus' fate. But His enemies evidently understood that Jesus had said that He would rise again from the dead after three days. Often, those who reject the message have greater fears that there might be a haunting truth to it than those who claim to believe it. They took extra precautions to guard against it. However, they could not permanently fight off God. This is how the Scriptures describe the closing moments of this part of the story:

At the place where Jesus was crucified, there was a garden, and in the garden a new tomb, in which no one had ever been laid. . . . They laid Jesus there.

Early on the first day of the week, while it was still dark, Mary Magdalene went to the tomb and saw that the stone had been removed from the entrance. So she came running to Simon Peter and the other disciple, the one Jesus loved, and said, "They have taken the Lord out of the tomb, and we don't know where they have put him!"

So Peter and the other disciple started for the tomb. Both were running, but the other disciple outran Peter and reached the tomb first. He bent over and looked in at the strips of linen lying there but did not go in.

Then Simon Peter, who was behind him, arrived and went into the tomb. He saw the strips of linen lying there, as well as the burial cloth that had been around Jesus' head. The cloth was folded up by itself, separate from the linen.

Finally the other disciple, who had reached the tomb first, also went inside. He saw and believed. (They still did not understand from Scripture that Jesus had to rise from the dead.)

Then the disciples went back to their homes, but Mary stood outside the tomb crying. As she wept, she bent over to look into the tomb and saw two angels in white, seated where Jesus' body had been. . . . They asked her, "Woman, why are you crying?"

"They have taken my Lord away," she said, "and I don't know where they have put him." At this, she turned around and saw Jesus standing there, but she did not realize that it was Jesus.

"Woman," he said, "why are you crying? Who is it you are looking for?"

Thinking he was the gardener, she said, "Sir, if you have carried him away, tell me where you have put him, and I will get him."

Jesus said to her, "Mary." (John 19:41–42; 20:1–16)

What a moment that was—a moment that spanned the breadth of the four gardens. From the text in the garden, to the context in the desert; from the contest in the Garden of Gethsemane, to the contrast, indeed, the culmination, in the garden where they laid Him. He was Lord of the universe, yet He called this simple woman by her name. Everything suddenly bloomed with meaning. The story of life was now seen through the eyes of her risen Lord. It is no wonder that she reached out just to touch Him. God is personal, God is relational, and God sees in an eternal sense. The victory was that of Jesus over those who would silence Him, then and for centuries after. He not only spoke, He also called them by their names. That is the difference in our world of anger, hate, and rancor. Name-calling is the symptom of our breakdown. How can we fully enter into the wonder and exultation that must have now pulsated through the very beings of those who loved Him and followed Him and whose names He called so tenderly?

I was reading recently the following words of a historian as he described the day the Second World War ended.

Men wept, unable to restrain themselves. . . . Feelings pent up and damned behind the mounting walls of five successive torturing, introverted years, had to erupt. They welled up like gushing springs, they overflowed, they burst their banks, they tumbled unhindered and uncontrolled. Frenchmen with tears streaming down their faces kissed each other on both cheeks—the salute of brothers. They kissed the GI, they kissed everyone within range. The storm of emotion burst. Home and country beckoned, loved ones were waiting . . . loved ones . . . were calling across the gulf of absent years. Man was at his finest amidst the grandeur of this moment of liberation. A noble symphony arranged by the Great Composer had reached its thunderous finale and, as the last triumphal chord swelled into the hymn of Nations, man looked into the face of his Creator turned towards him, a vision of tenderness, mirrored for an instant by the purity of his own unrepressed torrent of joy and thankfulness. At such a moment, mountains move at the behest of man, he has such power in the sight of God.[11]

Only one who fought that war can truly understand what these words mean. A battleground had suddenly turned into a celebration of life, when mountains moved, flowers bloomed, weapons were put away, and the sound of loved ones' voices could be heard once more.

Only one who has known the bondage and enslavement of sin and the emptiness it brings can fully fathom the liberation of the cross and the glory of the resurrection—to hear His voice again. No wonder the world of Christian thought is so adorned with a wealth of music. They are the sounds of finding that there is more than just a garden.

When Jesus speaks and says, "I am the way the truth and the life," He claims what no other did. When He says, "My sheep listen to My voice; I know them, and they follow Me. I give them eternal life, and they shall never perish; no one can snatch them out of My hand," He speaks as no other does. The Bible says that though God has spoken to us through the prophets and the apostles, His climactic expression is in the person of His Son, Jesus Christ (see Heb. 1:1–2).

In the second chapter of the Book of Philippians, the apostle Paul says this of Jesus:

> Who, being in very nature God, did not consider equality with God something to be grasped, but made himself nothing, taking the very nature of a servant, being made in human likeness. And being found in appearance as a man, he humbled himself and became obedient to death—even death on a cross! Therefore God exalted him to the highest place and gave him the name that is above every name, that at the name of Jesus every knee should bow, in heaven and on earth and under the earth, and every tongue confess that Jesus Christ is Lord, to the glory of God the Father. (vv. 6–11)

This Jesus called Mary by name and asked her, "Why are you crying? What are you looking for?"

Author Ken Gire tells this lovely story. A little girl who lived at the edge of a forest wandered off one day into the woods and thought she would explore all the dark secrets of the forest. The farther she wandered, the denser it became, till she lost her bearings and could not find her way back. As darkness descended, fear gripped her, and all her screams and sobs only wearied her till she fell asleep in the woods. Friends, family, and volunteers combed the area and gave up in the thick of night. Early the next morning, as her father began his search afresh, he suddenly caught a glimpse of his little girl lying on a rock and, calling her by name, ran as fast as he could. She was startled awake and threw her arms out to him. Wrapped in his tight embrace, she repeated over and over, "Daddy, I found you!"[12]

Mary discovered the most startling truth of all when she came looking for the body of Jesus. She did not realize that the person she had found was the One who had risen and that He had come looking for her.

Perhaps if our naturalists would stop looking only for a gardener, they might be surprised at who they would find, or should I say, at who finds them. They might actually hear Him call them by name also and might truly understand the gardens and the deserts of this world for the first time.

He is not dead. He is alive in the best sense of the term. The celebration has begun.

ENDNOTES

Chapter 1: Climbing a Massive Wall

1. W. E. H. Lecky, *A History of European Morals from Augustus to Charlemagne,* II (London: Longmans Green & Co., 1869). Quoted by F. F. Bruce in *Jesus, Lord and Savior* (Downers Grove, Ill.: InterVarsity Press, 1986), 15.

2. Sir Walter Scott, "Patriotism: Innominatus" *The Oxford Book of English Verse 1250–1900* (Oxford: The Clarendon Press, 1924), as cited in Bartleby Collection of Columbia University, http://www.bartleby.com/101/547.html.

3. The speaker on that occasion was Rev. Sam Wolgemuth, president of Youth for Christ International. Mr. Wolgemuth's son, Robert, published my first book in 1991, *A Shattered Visage: The Real Face of Atheism* (Nashville: Wolgemuth & Hyatt). Since that night, Sam Wolgemuth has become a treasured and revered friend, a spiritual father—something I had never envisioned as one of hundreds sitting and listening to a preacher on a warm night in Delhi. He, too, remembers the evening. He recalls getting little response as only one person had come forward in that large auditorium. As it turned out, I was that one.

4. Charles Wesley, "And Can It Be," *Hymns of the Christian Life* (Harrisburg, Pa.: Christian Publications, 1978), 104.

Chapter 2: Addressing a Heavenly Home

1. C. S. Lewis, quoted in Elisabeth Elliot, *Discipline: The Glad Surrender* (Old Tappan, N.J.: Fleming H. Revell Co, 1960), 62.

2. Christopher Hitchens, quoted in Carla C. Engelbrecht, "Hitchens' talk controversial sparks debate," *Campus Times News* (University of Rochester), on-line edition, 13 November 1997, www.ct.rochester.edu.

3. This event is recorded as *Al-Miraj,* in Surah 17.1. It is very important to note that this one verse in the Koran, on which they base Mohammed's heavenly journey, doesn't actually specify whether this journey was literal or visionary. Interpreters are on opposite sides of what this night journey actually meant. Not the least of their challenges is that Mohammed's wife said he was by her side the whole night and never left her physically. Also of consternation to Muslim scholars is that a very similar episode exists in Zoroaster's legend of a heavenly journey, which predates Islam. Textual critics continue to battle over whether this story was borrowed by Islam.

4. Used by personal permission of Larry King.

5. Islam from the beginning was primarily predisposed toward one particular people. There is very little doubt that in its inception, Islam was a geopolitical reaction to the other groups around them. Even those sympathetic to Islam, such as Ali Dashti, the noted Iranian journalist, comment that the greatest miracle in Islam is that it gave Mohammed's followers an identity, something they had lacked as various warring tribal groups. The very language of the Koran is restrictive. To claim that Mohammed's only miracle was the Koran and then to state that one cannot recognize the miracle unless one knows the language makes a miracle anything but universal. How can a "prophet to the world" be so narrowly restricted to a language group? The Koran, it is said, is only inspired in the original language—no other language can bear the miracle. The narrowness of its ethnic appeal cannot be ignored.

6. G. K. Chesterton, "The House of Christmas," from Robert Knille, ed., *As I Was Saying* (Grand Rapids: William B. Eerdmans, 1985), 304–5.

Chapter 3: The Anatomy of Faith and the Quest for Reason

1. Thomas Nagel, *The Last Word* (New York: Oxford University Press, 1997), 130.

2. Stephen Neill, quoted in J. Oswald Sanders, *Spiritual Leadership* (Chicago: Moody Press, 1994), 15.

3. Matthew Parris, "The Rage of Reason," *(London) Times*, 22 May 1999, 22.

4. David Hume, *On Human Nature and the Understanding*, Anthony Flew, ed. (New York: Collier Books, 1962), 163.

5. Lewis Thomas, quoted by Henry Brand and Philip Yancey, *Fearfully and Wonderfully Made* (Grand Rapids: Zondervan, 1980), 25.

6. Chandra Wickramasinghe, quoted by Norman Geisler, A. F. Brooke, and Mark J. Keosh, *The Creator in the Courtroom* (Milford, Mich.: Mott Media, 1982), 149.

7. Francis Criek, *Life Itself* (New York: Simon and Schuster, 1981), 88.

8. Deepak Chopra, *The Seven Spiritual Laws of Success* (San Rafael, Calif.: Amber Allen Publishing, 1994), 68–69.

9. Quoted in David Grossman, "Trained to Kill," *Christianity Today*, 10 August 1998, 7.

Chapter 4: A Taste for the Soul

1. Elizabeth Barrett Browning, "Aurora Leigh," quoted in Ken Gire, *Windows of the Soul* (Grand Rapids: Zondervan, 1996), 39.

2. Ravi Zacharias, *Cries of the Heart* (Nashville: Word Publishing, 1998), 221.

3. Jon Krakauer, *Into Thin Air* (New York: Villard Books, 1996), 187–88.

4. David A. Brown, *A Guide to Religions* (London: SPCK, 1975), 148.

5. Douglas Coupland, *Life After God* (New York: Pocket Books, 1994), 338.

6. Chopra, *The Seven Spiritual Laws of Success*, 3.

7. Ibid., 98.

8. Ibid., 102.

9. This is also the very reason, I might add, that there came an upheaval in Hindu thinking. Later philosophers repudiated this notion of God being impersonal, and a flurry of teaching emerged in subsequent Hindu thought that led to the worship of personal gods. The Gita forms the most popular of the Hindu scriptures and is rife with songs of worship and praise directed toward a personal god.

10. See Radhakrishnan in his *Hindu View of Life* (New Delhi, India: Indus, 1993), and Pandit Nehru in his comment on Hinduism, quoted in Brown, *A Guide to Religions*, 63.

11. Paul Waitman Hoon, *The Integrity of Worship* (Nashville: Abingdon Press, 1971), 164.

12. Mary A. Lathbury and Alexander Groves, "Break Thou the Bread of Life," *Hymns of the Christian Life*, 411.

Chapter 5: Is God the Source of My Suffering?

1. Used by permission of Mark Triplett.

2. Peter Kreeft, *Making Sense Out of Suffering* (Ann Arbor, Mich.: Servant Books, 1986), 51.

3. David Hume, *Dialogues Concerning Natural Religion, Part 10*, Henry D. Aiken, ed. (New York: Hafner Publishing Co., 1963), 64.

4. J. L. Mackie, quoted by J. P. Moreland, "Reflections on Meaning in Life without God," *The Trinity Journal*, 9 NS (1984): 14.

5. Richard Dawkins, *Out of Eden* (New York: Basic Books, 1992), 133.

6. Richard Dawkins, "Viruses of the Mind," 1992 Voltaire Lecture (London: British Humanist Association, 1993), 9.

7. G. K. Chesterton, *Orthodoxy* (Garden City, N.Y.: Doubleday, 1959), 41.

8. Jean Paul Sartre, *Being and Nothingness* (New York: Pocket Books, 1984), 478.

9. From Angutarra Nikaya, 7.5, quoted in *Guide to the Tipitaka* (Bangkok: White Lotus Company, Ltd., 1993), 97.

10. John McCutcheon, "Christmas in the Trenches," Lyrics and music by John McCutcheon/Appalsongs (ASCAP), 1984.

11. Robertson McQuilkin, *A Promise Kept* (Wheaton, Ill.: Tyndale House Publishers, Inc., 1998), 18–19.

12. Ibid., 85.

13. Coupland, *Life After God*, 359.

14. Alvin Plantinga, "A Christian Life Partly Lived" in Kelly James Clark, ed., *Philosophers Who Believe* (Downers Grove, Ill.: InterVarsity Press, 1993), 73.

15. Philip Hallie, *Lest Innocent Blood Be Shed* (Philadelpia: Harper & Row, 1979), 2, cited by Elenore Stump in her essay "The Mirror of Evil" in Thomas V. Morris, ed., *God and the Philosophers* (New York: Oxford University Press, 1994), 244.

16. Ibid., 241–42.

17. Stump, "The Mirror of Evil," 240, 242.

18. Malcolm Muggeridge, *A Twentieth Century Testimony* (Nashville: Thomas Nelson, 1978), 72.

19. Elie Wiesel, quoted in Dennis Ngien, "The God Who Suffers," *Christianity Today*, 3 February 1997, 40.

Chapter 6: When God Was Silent

1. Quoted in Henry Parry Liddon, *Liddon's Bampton Lectures 1866* (London: Rivingtons, 1869), 148.

2. Fyodor Dostoevsky, *The Brothers Karamazov* (Garden City, N.Y.: International Collectors Library), Chapter 5: "The Grand Inquisitor."

3. C. S. Lewis, *The Lion, the Witch and the Wardrobe* (New York: Collier Books), 159–60.

4. Hafiz Ghulan Sarwar, *Muhammad: The Holy Prophet* (Lahore, Pakistan: Sh. Muhammad Ashraf, 1969), 195.

5. For those interested in following up on the most recent challenges, I

recommend reading the January 1999 issue of *Atlantic Monthly,* which contains a fascinating article on Koranic studies: "What Is the Koran," by Toby Lester, 43–56.

6. M. K. Gandhi, *Pathway to God,* compiled by M. S. Deshpande (Ahmedabad: Navajivan Publishing House, 1971), 8, 9, 23. See also M. K. Gandhi, *In Search of the Supreme,* vol. 2 (Ahmedabad: Navajivan Publishing House, 1961), 265ff.

7. Christopher Isherwood, ed., *Vedanta for Modern Man* (New York: New American Library, 1972), 246.

8. Robert Bolt, *A Man for All Seasons* (Toronto: Irwin Publishing, 1963), 82.

Chapter 7: Is There a Gardener?

1. Anthony Flew, "Theology and Falsification," in John Hick, ed., *The Existence of God* (New York: Collier Books, 1964), 225.

2. John Frame, *"God and Biblical Language: Transcendence and Immanence"* in J. W. Montgomery (Ed.), *God's Inerrant Word* (Minneapolis: Bethany Fellowship), 171.

3. William Hamilton, quoted in Matt Ridley, "Why Should Males Exist?" *US News and World Report,* 18 August 1997 http://www.usnews.com/usnews/issue/970818/18male.htm.

4. Edmund Gosse, *Father and Son* (New York: Penguin Books, 1907, 1989), 249–51.

5. Ibid., 16–17.

6. Martin Hengel, *Crucifixion: The Ancient World and the Folly of the Cross* (Philadelphia: Fortress Press, 1977), 86–88.

7. Hengel, *Crucifixion,* 89–90.

8. Fyodor Dostoevsky, *Crime and Punishment* (New York: Bantam Books, 1987), 20.

9. Henri Nouwen, quoted in Gire, *Windows of the Soul,* 85.

10. George Matheson, "O Love, That Wilt Not Me Go," *Hymns of the Christian Life*, 181.

11. P. R. Reid, *The Latter Days at Colditz* (London: Hodder and Stoughton, 1952), 226–27.

12. Gire, *Windows of the Soul*, 215.

JESUS AMONG OTHER GODS
YOUTH EDITION

In a world with so many religions, our youth may ask, "Why Jesus?" With an easy to read, yet penetrating style, apologetics scholar and popular speaker Ravi Zacharias clearly contrasts the truth of Jesus with the founders of Islam, Hinduism, and Buddhism, strengthening teenage believers and compelling them to share their faith with a seeking world.

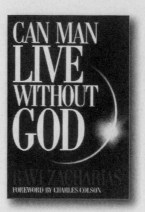

CAN MAN LIVE WITHOUT GOD

In this brilliant apologetic defense of the Christian faith—the likes of which we haven't seen since C. S. Lewis—Ravi Zacharias exposes the emptiness of life without God, discussing subjects including antitheism, the meaning of life, and the person of Jesus.

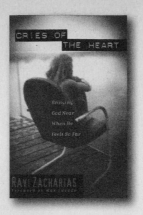

CRIES OF THE HEART

One of the greatest thinkers of our time covers new ground by exploring the deepest cries of the human heart. Through moving stories and relevant questions, Ravi Zacharias invites readers to join him in finding answers to the question: How can things be right when they feel so wrong?

DELIVER US FROM EVIL

In this compelling volume, Ravi Zacharias examines the mystery of evil. This brilliant writer and gifted teacher traces how secularization has led to a loss of shame, pluralization has led to a loss of reason, and privatization has led to a loss of meaning.